*An Insight into The Theology of African Initiated Churches (AIC)
Through a critical analysis of*

CHERUBIM & SERAPHIM EPISTEMOLOGY

C & S is a rapidly growing AIC
John O Adegoke

CHERUBIM & SERAPHIM EPISTEMOLOGY
John O Adegoke

Paperback edition first published in Great Britain in 2024 by aSys Publishing

Printed in Nigeria by Concept Publications, Lagos.
conceptpublications@gmail.com Tel: +1 469 655 1225

Copyright © John O Adegoke, 2024
All rights reserved.

No part of this document may be reproduced or transmitted in any form or by any means, electronic, mechanical, photocopying, recording, or otherwise, without prior written permission from the author.

John O Adegoke has asserted his rights under 'the Copyright Designs and Patents Act 1988' to be identified as the author of this work.

ISBN: 978-1-913438-87-6
Published by aSys Publishing

CONTENTS

Dedication vii
Acknowledgments ix
Foreword xi
Endorsements vii
Preface xiv
Dedication xvi

Introduction 1
AIC Typology 14
    Ethiopian Churches 17
    Zionist Churches 20
    Messianic Churches 24
    New Charismatic Churches 25
AIC Swot Analysis 27
    Spiritual Renewals 27
    Integrated Worship 29
    Inculturation 30
    Perceived Weaknesses 34
        Polygamy 35
        Pro Old Testament 42
        Old Testament Taboos 44
        Schism 45
        Paganism 47

Back to basics 50
    A Word of Caution 60
    Life cycle of the church 61
    The Rapture 63

The Mission of Cherubim & Seraphim Church 67
    Belief in supernatural powers 69
    The Quest for thaumaturgy 70
    Denominational Gifts and Specialisations 72
        Deliverance and Healing 74
        Faith 76
        Prayer and fasting 77
    Sprinkling and anointing 82
        The Essence of Prayer 83
        Evangelism 84
        Praise and Worship 85
    Places of prayer 88
    Understanding of pneumatology in C & S Epistemology ... 91
    Angelology in C & S Theology 96

Founders of Cherubim & Seraphim Church 101
    Moses Orimolade Tunolase 110
    Captain Christiana Abiodun Emmanuel 114
    A Tale of Two Missions 116
    The United Cherubim & Seraphim Society 117
    The Divided Cherubim and Seraphim Society 120
    Who founded Cherubim & Seraphim Society? 124
    The Reunited Society 126

Doctrines and Doctrinal Formations 129
  The Original Five Doctrinal Statements of C & S 129
  The Tabula Rasa Approach 131
  Implied Doctrinal Statements 132
    The Bible 133
    The Trinity 133
    The Creeds 134
    The Sacraments 134
    Water Consecration 135
    Transubstantiation 135
    Priesthood of Believers 136
    Concept of Salvation 136
    Predestination & Election 137
    Supernatural Powers 137
    Robing in white at worship 138
    Uniformity 143
  The sanctity of our Prayer Houses 147

Mode of Ministry 153
  The Ephesian 5-Hierarchy Ministry 153
    The Apostles 158
    The Prophets 158
    The Evangelists 161
    The Pastors 162
    The Teachers 162
  Ministerial Foundation in the C & S 163
  Women ministry in the C & S 165

The Cherubim & Seraphim Liturgy 170
    Believers' Baptism 181

Uniqueness of C & S Epistemology 183
    Hygiene codes 183
    Participative Worship 186
    The Amen factor 187
    Eschatology Scenarios 192
    The Prophetic Ministry 193
    Ringing of Bells 194
    Regularities and Irregularities 195
    The significance of Numbers 197

The C & S Under the Microscope 206
    Strengths 207
    Weaknesses 214
    Opportunities 224
    Threats 227

Conclusions 229

Bibliography 241

About the Book/Author 245

FOREWORD

Elder John Adegoke who oversees the Unification of Cherubim & Seraphim Churches, Europe Chapter is an individual that enjoys my tremendous respect because of his humility, dedication and for being on the same page with me at all times on my vision for expansion of our Church vertically and horizontally. I have read the manuscript over and over again and found every page epistemically infectious.

There is no doubt that some of the narratives have given rise to controversy. The Author himself acknowledges this fact and Readers who can spot such controversies are free to raise questions to the Author or in a suitable platform for clarifications. A meaningful dialogue on matters of controversy and grey areas in the book would unfold greater understanding of the C & S Epistemology and lead to consensus among us; and ultimately lead to the enhancement of our mission in proclaiming the Gospel of Christ.

In my view, we have now found that Satan has been employing the following "manias" to create division amongst us: title-mania, office-mania, position-mania, jealousy-mania, money mania and ego-mania. None of these can lead to salvation and eternal life. I urge those involved in promoting any of these manias to pull a break.

I recommend this book to every Seraph to convince all that we are the Salt and the Light of the world.

His Most Eminence, Most Elder Apostle Prophet (Dr.) Solomon A. Alao, JPil (SPIRITUAL PAUL) A.C.I.I, A.I.I.N, FINST, D, MNIN, FIAMN, QUAM,D.D

(The Supreme Head (Olori) C&S Unification Church, World wide).

ACKNOWLEDGEMENTS

With much gratefulness, I like to mention the name of Apostle Tunde Ogunkunle of Eternal Sacred Order of the Cherubim & Seraphim Church, Lagos Secretary General Emeritus of the Unification Council of Cherubim & Seraphim Churches who provided the map of Moses Orimolade's itinerary missionary journey from Ikare up and down the country of Nigeria. Secondly, Most Senior Apostle 'Dayo Adebayo of Holy Temple of Christ Cathedral C & S, Fadeyi, Lagos who supplied Parts I and II of the history of Moses Orimolade in the C & S Forum, from where I drew additional details of the history of our Great Leader. Third, I like to thank my children, Yetunde, Ibironke and Oluseyi in addition to family and friends who motivated me for many years before ending the serial writings that led to the publication of this book. Kudos to Yetunde especially who patiently undertook detailed reading and editing of the manuscript, though over several months! Kudos also to Ibironke who contributed immensely to producing the graphics and IT inputs.

To the Supreme Head (Olori) of the Unification of Cherubim & Seraphim Churches, Worldwide, His Most Eminence Prophet Dr Solomon Adegboyega Alao, who, despite his busy schedules consented and found time to write the FOREWORD to the book, I say thank you very much Sir. To Professors Clinton Ryan and Isaac Ojutalayo; Dr Hermion (Ayo) Harris who have read and endorsed the authenticity of the author's exegesis throughout the book from their academic perspectives I say, God bless you all. Finally, to all readers and prospective readers, I pray that your reading of the book (with or without comments) will bring you all abundant blessings and the betterment of the Cherubim & Seraphim Epistemology in particular, and greater propagation of the Gospel of Christ in general.

ENDORSEMENTS

The author of this volume, John Adegoke, reminds me of Apostle Paul. His commitment to Ministry, Mission and the Unity of The Christian Church are the mandates that have been driving passion of his life for many decades.

His intention as can be seen in this work, is that through the Church, with her many denominations, should be united to make known the manifold wisdom of God to rulers and authorities in the earthly and heavenly realms.

John Adegoke writes out of the vast ocean of his experience as an activist, academic, apostle and leader. He writes out of a heart that expresses sorrow for the division in the Christ Church and he challenges individual Christian and the whole Church. Locally, nationally and internationally to repent of the sin of disunity.

In this work there is a clear call for the Church to return to its original mandate of being in the world- for being salt and light in our confused and violent age. In his view the true church will have set backs, but she will always survive her enemies. The promise of the Church's founder, Jesus Christ promised ''I will build my Church and the gates of hell shall not prevail (Matt 16:18).

The visible Church

The Church of Jesus Christ is still in the process of being built. People are still coming to know Jesus Christ as the Redeemer and Saviour. Therefore, we can say the Church is her true self when she confesses Jesus Christ as the Son of the living God, live in obedience in His commands and have Spiritual effect upon humanity, beginning in the Community where she is founded and having impact on the whole world. The message of the Church is for the whole world and will not be confined to by boundaries, barriers colour or race.

The contents of this volume further emphasise that the LORD Jesus Christ is not only the founder of the Church, but He is also the Head of the Church. The Church is composed of all His true servants. The Church Theologically is spoken of in two parts

1. The Church Militant

2. The Church Triumphant

God invested in Jesus Christ all power and authority for the Government of His Church and Jesus Christ in His commission to His disciples authorised them to preach, teach, plant congregation, and heal the sick throughout the world. To each of these Churches or congregations, He has given all needful authority for administration, order, discipline, education, evangelism and worship.

The author has mentioned a number of denominations structures, including The Cherubim and Seraphim Church. He states clearly that The Cherubim and Seraphim is based on Ephesians 4:11 model of ministry.

It is my distinct joy and privilege to recommend this work to Canada Christian College and School of Graduate Theological Studies of the Degree of Doctor of Literature. It is my hope and prayer that all who read this volume will be blessed by its contents and become more aware of the AICs.

Clinton L Ryan, Th.D.

(Programme Coordinator:Canada Christian College and School of Graduate Theological Studies - United Kingdom and Caribbean.)

I couldn't agree with you more! This book by Dr. John Adegoke is an incredibly insightful and thought-provoking read. As an insider, Dr. Adegoke gives readers a unique perspective on the Epistemology of the Cherubim and Seraphim Church and its relevance to other denominations that the organization is not a cult but functions under the guidance of the Holy Spirit.

All are encouraged to look at our culture's benefits and not neglect our heritage. The book is filled with valuable information that would interest historians, scholars, and anyone interested in the Theology of African Initiated Churches.

One thing that particularly stood out to me was Dr. Adegoke's emphasis on the importance of culture and traditions about Scripture. He highlights how culture and religion are intertwined in the history of Europeans and encourages us as Africans to be proud of our heritage.

The twelve chapters are all incredibly relevant and provide a better understanding of the Cherubim and Seraphim Church, a denomination I also belong to.

Overall, I highly recommend this publication to anyone looking to learn something new and gain a deeper understanding of the Epistemology of the Cherubim and Seraphim Church.

Isaac O.O. Ojutalayo D. Min; D. Lt; D.D

(Principal: All Nations Bible College and School of Theological Studies London, in affiliation with Canada Christian College and School of Graduate Theological Studies).

PREFACE

This Book is the product of requests by many listeners to my casual and formal utterances over many years as a Pastor. I thank God that it finally emerges after many years of inevitable distractions including Pastoral Duties, Committee Meetings, Travels, College Assignments, Lack of Facilities, Computer and IT illiteracy. Family Challenges and even periods of ill health.

The Book is a collection and collation of a few out of many materials acquired over many years. No wonder my house very often became untidy due to paperwork scattered in unappropriate places; and leading to repeated reprimands from my wife and children!

Although the Book is principally on C & S Epistemology, the first two chapters are given to satisfying enquiring minds as to what prompted the emergence of Cherubim & Seraphim Church. The initial chapters show how the Holy Spirit moved across many nations during the late nineteenth and early twentieth centuries and to show that the emergence of Cherubim & Seraphim was not of a human design but of divine creation. Readers who are more interested about the C & S Epistemology are advised to start reading from Chapter 3 of the Book. The first two Chapters are more of academic interest but reading the whole book surely leads the reader to greater understanding of the Epistemology.

Although many of the materials employed derive from Desk and Field Research, but most are spiritually and experientially acquired and the result of penning some details of dreams and revelations over many years. This is the very reason that I am equipped and ready to expatiate on any issue of grey areas throughout this narrative. The Author is ready for dialogue either formally or informally. I pray and wish my Readers every good wish and blessings for a greater understanding of the C & S Epistemology.

John O Adegoke (December 2024).

DEDICATION

It is my pleasure to dedicate this book to my late wife. Victoria Fehintola Adegoke who passed away 3 years ago after being together with me as an intimate friend, inseparable partner and wife for 57 years. She was a rock behind my every move and did contribute immensely to my success and happiness. May her soul rest perfectly in the bosom of our Saviour, Jesus Christ.

The book is also a humble homage to my late mum, Deborah Adegoke who taught me how to read the Bible in my infancy; and to my dad, Joshua Adegoke whose ambition for me was to train as a priest in the Anglican ministry. I finally ended up in Cherubim & Seraphim ministry with the support of my wife and children! May the rest of my life serve as fulfilment of their prayers and wishes for me.

CHAPTER 1

INTRODUCTION

The title 'African *Initiated* Churches' (AICs), actually started with the middle initial as 'Independent' and later developed to other initials: Instituted, Indigenous and lately, International. The reasons for these initials will be explained in chapter two dealing with the AIC in their African context.

This book takes a closer look at one of the AIC's—the Cherubim and Seraphim (C&S) Church. which has grown organically over the years with more oral rather than written guidance on doctrine, code of conduct, structures and systems. This book attempts to document the epistemology of C&S from an 'insider' perspective, addressing many myths and misconceptions of the spiritual basis and practices of the C&S church by academics and other Christian denominations. This has been done in the context of recognising why and how those misconceptions have been perpetuated by impersonators which under a non-centralised structure of growth have been left unchecked. This book aims to capture ongoing internal debates on necessary reforms to promote unity, standardisation and relevance to God's Kingdom Mission within today's advancing society and proposes some necessary steps to effect the transformational change required.

'Cherubim & Seraphim' are the names given to the highest ranks of Angels surrounding the throne of the Almighty God. In fact, the throne of God is not made by hand but by the coming together of Angels who are none other than the Cherubim and

Introduction

Seraphim. Surprisingly, many Christians seem to know little or nothing about Cherubim and Seraphim. But many of them sing the hymn, one verse of which reads:

> *Holy Holy Holy, All the saints adore Thee,*
> *Casting down their golden crowns around the glassy sea;*
> *Cherubim and Seraphim, falling down before Thee,*
> *Which were, and art, and evermore shall be.*

This hymn was composed by Reginald Heber (1783-1826). He was an English Anglican Bishop (Bishop of Calcutta), a man of letters and hymn writer, who died at the age of 44. This hymn derives from the apocalyptic Scriptures and has been sung in the church even before the Cherubim & Seraphim Church was founded! Heber recognised through inspiration that Cherubim and Seraphim are the highest ranking angels that surround the throne of God and form the heavenly choir singing the praise of God without ceasing day and night. This is one of the favourite hymns in the church and often sung as an Introit during divine worship in the C & S churches. The Old Testament has several references to Cherubim but only one reference was made to the Seraphim in the sixth chapter of Isaiah where it is shown that the Seraphim have free access to the throne of God. Psalms eighty and ninety-nine particularly show the affinity and proximity of the Cherubim to the throne of the Almighty God. Amongst the ranks of angels, therefore, it can be seen that the Cherubim and Seraphim are the closest to the throne of grace.

'Epistemology' means the theory of method or grounds of knowledge. It derives from the Greek word, 'episteme' meaning knowledge; and 'logos' meaning Word of God and second person of the Trinity. It signifies the inquiry into the nature of knowledge and its acquisition through senses, reason etc. Empiricism, rationalism, scepticism etc are all epistemological stances. Epistemology in this context seeks to explain what practices are peculiar to the Cherubim & Seraphim that are not common anywhere else and why. In relation to the Cherubim & Seraphim, it is an offering to global Christianity for the enrichment of ecumenism in the pursuit of greater effectiveness in Christian missiology. This is not to be interpreted as claiming any perfection or superiority in our offerings (for all have fallen short of the glory of God) but simply trying on the other hand to provide a framework within which our Christian theology can be enhanced and made more effective through patient listening, learning and engaging in constructive dialogues.

In a review of Callan Slipper's booklet 'Enriched by the Other: a spiritual guide to receptive ecumenism[1] Stephen Copson explains that 'that unity is not a by-product of Christian activity but its engine. It is not an optional extra but something that, if missing, impairs the Christian witness. Here is the impetus for theological discussion and practical discipleship that flows out of a mutual indwelling in the Triune God. Theology becomes an exploration together of the riches of God and mission is the reconciling people of God acting to reconcile the world.

Receptive Ecumenism is that encouragement to be committed to one another to listen, reflect and appreciate what others have to offer, both individuals and ecclesial communities. The generous God scatters gifts among His people, for their edification and mutual sharing. In accepting the gifts, people are drawn deeper into the life of the Giver. This is perhaps easier to achieve at the

---

1 Slipper, Slipper 'Enriched by the Other: a spiritual guide to receptive ecumenism', Grove Books 139

Introduction

level of individual believers than for blocs in formal conversations. The activity must extend beyond the traditional ecumenical partners, and embrace more recently emerging traditions that may not as yet recognise the value of 'the other'. This book further encourages exploration of what do you and your tradition bring to the feast? Over the past decades readers will recognise cross-fertilisation in styles of worship, aspects of prayer and practical social action. Many congregations consist of people whose stories of faith started in another denomination, or none. Are the gifts that individuals bring necessarily the same as those that the ecclesial body offers? To accept a gift is not to put it on display but to put it to work, so what sort of individuals and what sort of denominations might emerge from this bi-lateral conversation?' Callan Slipper is noted for his passion for ecumenism both in word and in deed. Apart from his writings, he has promoted many ecumenical initiatives attended by a good variety of delegates from a variety of denominations and participants. More of his kind are needed today for the enhancement of church mission and evangelism.

This book has been written for many reasons. The author is aware of the negative perception and sometimes adverse publicity labelled against the Cherubim & Seraphim and other 'white garment' churches in contemporary Christian discourse. This book is not necessarily aimed to put up any concerted defence with a view to eradicate the pseudo stigma with which Christians from other denominations and backgrounds have described these churches originating from Africa. It is more of an attempt to help sceptics to understand where the African Christian believer is coming from culturally and spiritually and how he has travelled through the often thorny spiritual pilgrimage to arrive at a credible and fulfilled Christian mission.

Cherubim & Seraphim Epistemology

Many ecclesiastical analysts would jump to wrong and unholy conclusions with little or no knowledge of African culture and worship, and without sufficient in-depth study of African churches. Such sceptics have described African churches as sects, cults or even pagans. But a few who have taken time to study without prejudice, and understood that the African as a holistic believer and worshipper, would become aware that the worship of God cannot be bottled in a single cultural setting. To so believe is to restrict the preaching of the gospel of Christ to a 'closed shop' perspective or, to a narrow cultural setting. In Christ, there is no East or West. Paul the Apostle explained that:

'I am made all things to all men, that I might by all means save some.'

He learnt to reconcile with differing cultures as he explained:

'For though I be free from all men, yet have I made myself servant unto all, that I might gain the more. And unto the Jews I became as a Jew, that I might gain the Jews; to them that are under the law, as under the law, that I might gain them that are under the law; to them that without law, as without law, (being not without law to God, but under the law to Christ.) that I might gain them that are without law. To the weak became I as weak, that I might gain the weak; I am made all things to all men . . . ' (I Cor 1:19-22)

For this reason amongst others, Christianity could legitimately be seen as, African, Asian, European, Latin American or as in any other cultural contexts. This exposition, therefore, aims on the other hand to put the case as it is from the background and knowledge of the Scriptures and how they relate to people of differing class, tribes, tongues and cultures.

Introduction

The second reason is that many outsiders have written volumes about the Cherubim & Seraphim in particular and about Aladura churches in general. I see them as 'outsiders' because they are academics, sociologists, anthropologists and theologians from the background of different Christian denominations. Most of these authors have come as researchers with or without prejudices. It is not possible for most of them to gain perfect knowledge of the doctrines and culture of the AIC. They are prone to follow a pre-determined agenda and within the limits of their work, rush to some conclusions which might look convincing to an outsider; but to an insider, as non authentic. Hence this attempt to narrate the story as an insider and provide the opportunity for outsiders to hear evidence from the horses' mouth that can neither be faulted nor ignored.

Whilst an attempt is made to spotlight the virtues of C & S epistemology, every effort is also being made to look at the church from the outside perspective. With the level and depth of ecumenical involvement of the author, a catalogue of comments positive and negative have been noted and these coupled with the author's own internal experience have led to a critical appraisal of the strengths and weaknesses of the church, the threats that need to be confronted and debunked; the opportunities that are open to the church in the mass market of mission and evangelism in which we operate. It is through such analysis that this epistemology can achieve the desired aim of aiding effective evangelism and promoting *missio dei*, the mission of God.

Cherubim & Seraphim prides herself as biblically based and that there is nothing 'African' in her doctrines and theology that are not first 'Christian'. African worldview is not different to the Semitic and is essentially different to European, Asian, Latin American or any other cultural worldview. The same can be said of African Christianity in relation to the others. There are, therefore, global varieties in our Christianity but we seek (or should seek) unity in our diversity by celebrating those common threads that bind us together in the faith. We should do this more than pinpointing the differences in which each culture seeks to position itself in a 'holier than thou' perception. Perhaps God created us differently to test our tolerances and understanding between one another; black or white; pink or brown; blue or yellow! In whatever colour or culture we fall into, therefore, we should learn to celebrate our diversity and be thankful for the common threads that bind us together: our acceptance that Jesus is the son of God, the Saviour of the world from their sins, our renouncing of the devil and all his works, our baptism into the life, death and resurrection of Christ, our affirmation of the Apostles Creed, the Nicene Creed and the Athanasian Creed. Interpretation and understanding of Bible narratives and from there, interpretation and understanding of Christianity can be different from culture to culture.

Looking at Western Christianity, there are varieties of beliefs and theologies. There is the Roman Catholicism, the Orthodox, the Anglican, the Methodist, the Baptist, the Quakers, the Salvation Army, the Pentecostals, the Charismatics and many others. In each of these, there is always a focus on a particular point of the message of the Gospel of Christ. We may call this specialisation in Christianity. By the same token, the AICs have specialisations one way or the other. The chapter on AIC typology will further explain these specialisations. There are some who put emphasis on independence, some on indigenisation, some on purity and non ritualistic theology, some on prosperity, some on evangelisation, but the C & S in particular focuses on deliverance and healing ministry more than anything else. A close study of the indigenous

Introduction

hymns of the C & S will confirm that the ethos of the church is centred on deliverance, healing and worship of the Almighty God, and singing His praises as the angels do in heaven.

This book, therefore, seeks to highlight the methodologies employed to achieving this purpose. It will explain to the world what the C & S is, and what it is not, as perceived by some external observers and critics. The C & S has so far, resisted being driven to populist tendencies in worship in order to attract more adherents. Future modernity in the church cannot be ruled out but any reformation or aspect of it must be carried out within the context of the ministry and the ethos of the church which must essentially remain intact. As Paul did point out

'According to the grace of God which is given unto me, as a wise masterbuilder, I have laid the foundation, and another buildeth thereon. But let every man take heed how he buildeth thereupon. For other foundation can no man lay than that is laid, which is Jesus Christ.' (I Cor 3:10-11)

As Moses Orimolade, the anointed prophet of God has laid the foundation of preaching, deliverance and healing ministry, any subsequent builder on this foundation should always be measured against the Orimolade template, or the original foundation which was laid at the beginning. Any substantive deviation from this foundation will not have any claim to be counted among the Cherubim & Seraphim.

It cannot be denied that this foundation has been, in places, adulterated as a result of insufficient level of organisation and discipline; yet the core ethos of the church can be identified from her statement of doctrines and practices as will be outlined in a later chapter.

Cherubim & Seraphim Epistemology

From the similarity of African and Semitic cultures, it may not be arrogant to claim that some biblical narratives have clearer explanations in African culture than any other. Predestination for instance, of the struggle for power in conception, of the birth and lives of twin brothers, Esau and Jacob (Gen. 25) has almost common occurrence in African culture whilst the same narrative may pose interpretative and doctrinal problems to other cultures. It is difficult to perceive the reason why God would allow the unborn creatures to engage in a power struggle even in the womb of their mother; and to warn the mother of their predestinations. One would tend to ask where the justice can be discerned in this struggle, knowing that our God is a God of justice and of peace! But God should be perceived as 'Almighty' meaning, 'all powerful' with the power to do what He wants to do, when He wants to do it and how He wants to do it, without questioning or screening for justice! It is this question of justice that puts the question mark on the pride of God to describe Himself as the God of Abraham, the God of Isaac and the God of Jacob variously in the Old Testament.

If there should be justice as perceived from human wisdom, God should have been described as the God of Abraham, the God of Isaac and the God of Esau (instead of Jacob). In the modern course of justice, Esau, being the elder of the twins could have legitimately and justifiably brought an injunction in the court of law to prevent the name of Jacob from being so laboriously mentioned and celebrated in the scriptures instead of his own name! Such an injunction would have resulted in changing the slogan to 'The God of Abraham, the God of Isaac and the God of Esau' But theologically, our God is Almighty. The shift of preference has to do with predestination and with divine architecture. God's thoughts are higher than human thoughts and anything God does or approves must stand and cannot be challenged.

Introduction

Because of the similarity between Semitic and African cultures, there are some Biblical narratives that have deep rooted authenticity in African culture where on the other hand, they have very little or no meaning in many other cultures. An example is when Jesus expressed himself in African culture as he described the habit of market women:

'good measure, pressed down, and shaken together, and running over' (Lk. 6:38).

Most African women would readily recognise this practice in the marketplace; whilst the interpretation and understanding of it could pose problems in some other cultures. In Africa, some foodstuffs are sold in bowls and/or tins as standards of measure especially soft commodities like cassava powder or yam powder, rice or beans. Buyers are usually allowed to help themselves to measure from the vast supply into their own containers. When they do, some experienced buyers tend to overload the bowls by 'pressing down and shaking' the bowl to ensure that the quantity bought is maximised or 'runs over'. The 'running over' varies, depending on the individual buyer's experience. In other words, the technique is essentially aimed to take more than average from the seller, or to cheat the seller. Heavily built women can by this method maximise quantity bought than can smaller women.

Whilst most interpretations assume that 'the more you give, the more you receive back' the author, who is conversant with and emanates from African culture thinks that Jesus saw this as an unfair deal to the seller; and tries to warn the greedy buyer that such a practice of unfairness would be returned to her in judgement; because whereas the seller budgeted the quantity for sale at an average price, some skilful buyers invariably succeded in gaining greater quantity and subsequently resulting in profit shortfall to the seller. This interpretation is synonymous to the 'golden rule' (Matt. 7:12) and perhaps more philosophical that warns:

'Therefore all things whatsoever you would that men should do to you, do you even so to them; for this is the Law and the Prophets'

Apparently, if the buyer puts her feet in the shoes of the seller, the latter would gain more profit to the detriment of the former. It is therefore a warning and not an encouragement based on the maxim 'do unto others, what you would like them to do unto you'. This is a different interpretation of the narrative as compared with the prosperity gospelling perspective, which gives the impression that 'the more you give in donations, the more you receive back' and thus motivating donors to double up their donations!

Such methods of selling and buying is not common outside the Semitic, Asian and African cultures, where in modern times, quantities of commodities are predetermined by mechanical measuring before, or at the point of selling. In such a case, there cannot be room to take advantage either by the buyer or by the seller. As both quantity and price are predetermined, a fair deal is ensured, undue advantage by either party is impossible and haggling is out of the question.

Finally this book is intended to provide sufficient basic information as a manual for the inquisitive and as a reference point for academic research. It is hoped that the book will provide sufficient Biblical evidence for our fellow Christians from the background of Black Pentecostals especially from America and the West Indies, who have often been prejudiced against Africans as 'second class' Christians. This also applies to our fellow Christians of other denominations in Nigeria, who due to those imposters that have

Introduction

deviated from the foundation and used the name of C&S as to mask non-Christian practices and sources of spiritual powers, at times question whether C&S is even Christian! It is also intended to cover adequate tuition as catechism for the young members of C & S and for new adherents to the faith. There are doctrinal practices that need to be explained and this book will attempt to cover as much as the author can gather through personal experience coupled with desk and field research about the Cherubim & Seraphim doctrines and practices in particular, and of the African Indigenous Churches in general.

There is no doubt that the book will be seen as rather short in bibliography because the Cherubim and Seraphim, like many other AICs, emanates from the oral tradition. Stories have been passed down the generations about the beginnings, the development and growth of the churches like the C & S. Most of the evidence, therefore, will be deduced from practices in worship, liturgy and day to day living. This means that references to certain claims will have to be taken in good faith. It should be pointed out that certain aspects of this writing originate from recollections from the author's dreams and visions from time to time (not because these recollections are imaginative, but as guidance to highlight the essentials) and hence the expositions are spiritually inspired.

Like most AIC theology, the practical theology of the C & S has turned a blind eye on streamlined liberal theology and aspects of modernity especially prevalent in Western Christianity, but rather, it has concentrated mainly on interpreting the Scripture in its entirety from both Old and New Testaments. Whilst Mosaic laws are not forgotten, but the core message of the Gospels incorporating the essence and dispensation of love has been given higher credibility in worship and praise. Hence, the superiority of the

Cherubim & Seraphim Epistemology

New Testament is highlighted in the AIC theology without discarding the Old in its entirety. Sacrifices of animals, birds and of blood generally are replaced by the once and for all sufficient oblation of our Lord Jesus Christ. On the other hand, the richness of the ministry of prophets like Elijah and Elisha, the wealth of prayer models afforded by the psalms and other spiritual aspects of the Old Testament are retained and effectively utilised for greater optimisation of biblical resources and delivery of prayer efficacy.

CHAPTER 2

AIC TYPOLOGY[2]

It will be helpful to explain what AIC stands for. The middle initial especially has been changed from time to time to describe the kind of AIC under discussion. African Initiated Churches, according to Harold Turner, are founded by Africans in Africa primarily for Africans.[3] This group of churches have developed throughout Africa, south of the Sahara, from the South through to the East and West coasts of the continent with pronounced diversity of doctrine and culture. The middle initial has been described as 'Independent' to signify the diversity in theology and administration at the point of schism between the parent missionary church and the 'independent' African wing which happen to believe differently. These churches continue to worship in the same way as the parent churches but change the rules on such questions like polygamy, feminism and ordination.

This explanation does not suit the other churches who actually developed through the call of Prophets whose ministries developed to full fledged churches. For such churches, the middle initial has been variously described as Indigenous, Initiated, Instituted and lately as International.[4] The initial 'International' was suggested by a Dutch

---

2 Adegoke, John O, *How central is prayer for healing in the mission of African Indigenoous Churches?* MA Assignment, Module 403, 2005

3 Turner, H.W., *A typology for African Religious Movements*, Journal of Religions in Africa, 1967, p17

4 Harris, Hermione, *Yoruba in Diaspora*, palgrave macmillan, USA 2006, p3

scholar and sociologist, Ter Haar's because according to her, the AICs have now planted churches in most countries and hence, have assumed international status. The author, however, prefers the term 'Initiated' because it especially resonates the fact that Africans have the guts and inspiration to contribute to the global Christian mission and also because it is the preference of the World Council of Churches.

The "three self"[5] formula for indigenisation put forward by missionary leaders, Henry Venn and Rufus Anderson in the mid nineteenth century—self-governing, self-supporting and self-propagating—was automatically and effortlessly achieved by the AICs long before this goal was realised by European mission churches.[6] During the late 1970's, John Mbiti[7] complained that

> *'it is utterly scandalous for so many Christian scholars in the old Christendom to know so much about heretical movements in the second and third centuries, when so few of them know anything about Christian movements in areas of the younger churches.*[8]

---

5 The **three-self formula** or **three-self principle** is a missiological strategy to establish indigenous churches. Its principles are: self-governance, self-support (i.e., financial independence from foreigners), and self-propagation (i.e., indigenous missionary work). It was first coined in the late-19th century by various missions theorists

6 Bosch, David J, *Transforming Mission*, New York, Orbis Book, 1995, p331

7 Mbiti, John S, *New Testament Eschatology in an African background*, London SPCK, 1978, p32

8 Mbiti is quoted in Bediako, *Christianity in Africa*, p154

AIC Typology

The position is now different and excellent books are now written about the growth of Christianity in Africa, south of the Sahara with significant contribution to the growth by the AIC. The author agrees with Philip Jenkins when he argues that:

> *'rapid growth is occurring in non-traditional denominations that adapt Christian belief to local tradition, groups that are categorised by titles like "African Indigenous Churches." Their exact numbers are none too clear, since they are too busy baptising newcomers to be counting them very precisely. By most accounts, membership in Pentecostal and independent churches already runs into the hundreds of millions, and congregations are located in precisely the regions of fastest population growth. Within a few decades, such denominations will represent a far larger segment of global Christianity, and just conceivably a majority.'*[9]

It is very difficult to classify the different churches that constitute the AIC. Different writers have attempted to group and regroup according to different characteristics but no one has been able to come up with an accurate classification. It is understood that the number of church denominations are in thousands across Africa who profess minor differences. Part of the problem of classification stems from the absence of any defined statement of doctrines for these churches. Most of these churches developed through the calling and ministry of their prophets. These prophets were called mostly by visions or through dreams. Through these media, they were given divine instructions to preach or to do the work of healing. As they were called by the Holy Spirit, there could not be written documentations to guide their ministries as would

---

9 Jenkins, Philip, *The Next Christendom, The Coming of Global Christianity*, Oxford, OUP, 2002, p7/8

be expected of organised structures found in Western traditional churches.

It is believed that even till today, many of the AICs have no written doctrines, and of those who have, there are always generalisations which lack uniqueness. There must be some distinctiveness to affirm a separate identity. Because of the lack of distinctiveness between similar churches, blanket labels have become convenient to describe them. An example is the 'white garment churches' which in West Africa consist of Cherubim & Seraphim Churches, Church of the Lord Aladura, Celesial Church of Christ, Brotherhood of the Cross & the Star, Divine Prayer Society and some others. However, the following headings provide a rough guide to the various groups as classified by Sundkler[10]:

Ethiopian Churches

The AICs designated 'Ethiopian' are non-prophetic and lay no emphasis on the gifts of the Holy Spirit. They do not practise baptism by immersion and their worship services are non emotional. They do very little or no exorcism and are not interested in the menace of witches. They have fewer rules and regulations about the consumption of food and drink .There is little or no difference between them and their parent churches in worship, liturgies, clerical vestments and administrative structures. For survival, some of them have recently modified their worship styles to imitate those of the Pentecostals and Zionists in order to halt further decline in their membership. Ethiopianism is very common in Zimbabwe and South Africa, with a few in West Africa. To the Africans, Ethiopianism usually refers to the broad movement of

---

10 Sundkler, Bengt, *The Bantu Prophets in South Africa*, London, Lutterworth Press, 1948

AIC Typology

ecclesiastical independency in South Africa at the turn of the nineteenth century and hence defined in broader terms.

The successful resistance of European colonial power in Ethiopia, coupled with the historiography of the conversion of the Ethiopian Eunuch (Acts 8) and Psalm 68:31

'Princes shall come out of Egypt; Ethiopia shall soon stretch out her hands unto God'

are interpreted as a sign that the oppressed black people have a specially appointed place in God's plan for salvation. The fact that baby Jesus was taken to Egypt for refuge by divine instruction, coupled with the fact that it was prophesied by Hosea that *'Out of Egypt have I called my son'* gave Africa the pride of playing a leading role in the divine plan for salvation. The carrying of the cross of Christ by Simon of Cyrene was seen as a claim that Africa responded to Christ's message of salvation long before the European peoples did. This gave rise to a psychological sense of self confidence, self-esteem and responsibility for spreading God's kingdom in Africa.[11] Ethiopianism does not imply that any church from Ethiopia did plant churches in other parts of Africa.

Ethiopianism, therefore, is merely, in the context of the AIC, an expression of independency of newly created churches as a protest against certain doctrines and practices of their parent missionary churches. It should not be confused with the Ethiopian Orthodox Church which was in existence in Ethiopia, Nubia and Sudan before the emergence of Independent churches.

---

11 Daneel, Inus, *Quest for Belonging*, Harare, Mambo Press 1987, p38

Cherubim & Seraphim Epistemology

The following is an extract from the church web: "The Ethiopian Orthodox Church is one of the five so-called monophysite churches, characterised by their rejection of the Council of Chalcedon (451). In contrast to Chalcedon's doctrine that Christ is one person existing in two natures the Ethiopian Orthodox Church affirms that Christ's humanity cannot be separated from his divinity. After the incarnation the thoughts and actions of Jesus were those of a single unitary being. The Ethiopian Orthodox Church closely follows the precepts of the Old Testament. Church members are expected to be circumcised, to follow the dietary practices set out in the Old Testament, and observe Saturday as the Sabbath.

Christianity in Ethiopia dates back to the 4th century. It was brought to the region by a Christian captive, Frumentius, who later became Ethiopia's first bishop. Frumentius was consecrated by Athanasius the Great in Alexandria, an act which placed the Ethiopian church under the jurisdiction of the Coptic Church of Egypt. Monasticism was introduced towards the end of the 5th century by nine monks from Syria who are believed to have translated the Bible into the local language, Ge'ez. From the 7th century Ethiopia was cut off from the rest of the Christian world by the Islamic conquest of North Africa. Chronic skirmishes between Christians and Muslims led to the outbreak of civil war in the 16th century and the sacking of monasteries and the burning of churches. In the 17th century the conversion of the emperor to Roman Catholicism and the attempt to impose his faith on his subjects produced fierce resistance and the martyrdom of many thousands of Christians. In 1959 the Ethiopian church became independent from Egypt when an Ethiopian patriarch was elected."

The case for Ethiopianism has been weakened especially during the second part of the twentieth century. As the number of educated and articulate black people grows, many mainline churches have been forced to accept black people into leadership positions. Today, unlike half a century ago, there are African bishops, moderators and high ranking officials leading multiracial churches even in Southern Africa which suffered a long spell of apartheid in their political and religious history. This is a reversal of the experience of the Church Missionary Society in West Africa where the leadership of black people was successfully resisted by the white missionaries and leading to the downfall of Samuel Ajayi Crowther, the first black African bishop.[12] This is also a victory for the vision of Church Missionary Society's Henry Venn, who campaigned for self-supporting, self-governing and self-extending churches, a campaign which led to the consecration of Crowther as bishop on June 29th, 1864.[13] The churches identified under this heading include: In Southern Africa, African Methodist Episcopal Church, Thembu Church of Nehemiah Tile, Transkei Church of Christ.[14] In West Africa, United Africa Church.

Zionist Churches

Zionism is a term that covers churches which are described as 'Zionists' in Southern Africa. Opinions differ widely as to the most appropriate nomenclature for these types of churches. 'Zionist' is

---

12 Omoyajowo, Akin J, *An African Expression of Christianity*, ed Basil Moore, Black Theology, London, C Hurst & Company, 1973, P84

13 Beaumont, Mark, *MA Module 403, BCC Lecture Note 6, 2003/04, Henry Venn on planting self-supporting, self-governing and self-extending churches.*

14 Pretorius, H L, *Ethiopia stretches out her hands unto God*, Pretoria, University of Pretoria, 1993, p40

preferred by Sundkler in his original writing[15] because so many of the prophetic groups in Southern Africa are Zionist.[16] The word 'Zion' often features in their names and they have indigenised concepts of a kingdom of God in which the holy city of Zion occupies a focal position in their thoughts, either symbolically or in a concrete sense. Whilst Sundkler calls this group 'Zionist' type churches, Daneel calls them 'Spirit-type'[17] churches, because some prophetic movements specifically do not want to be considered Zionist, so that the designation is not general enough.

The Apostolic Faith Mission also comes under this description although there are some differences between 'Zionists' and 'Apostolics' but not as marked as with the Pentecostals. Both Zionists and Apostolics emphasise the working of the Holy Spirit including dreams, speaking in tongues, visions, prophecy and healing. However, they are not overly preoccupied with 'speaking in tongues' or glossolalia, which is the hallmark of classical Pentecostals, who regard it as the 'initial evidence' of the baptism with the Holy Spirit. [18] To the classical Pentecostals, speaking in tongues confers, assuredly, the privilege of being saved. Hence, when a Pentecostal asks the question, 'Are you saved?' he actually means 'Have you spoken in tongues?' The speaking in tongues, therefore, becomes central to theology of the Pentecostals.

---

15 Sundkler, Bengt, *Bantu Prophets of South Africa*, London, Lutterworth Press, 1948, p302

16 Daneel, Inus, *Quest for Belonging*, p39

17 MacRobert, Iain, *The Black Roots and White Racism of Early Pentecostalism in the USA,* Basingstoke, Macmillan 1988, p60

18 Turner, Max, *Power from on High, The Spirit is Israel's Restoration and Witness in Luke-Acts,* Sheffield, SAP, 2000, P446ff.

AIC Typology

In West Africa, 'Zionism' covers Aladura and Prophetic churches like The Apostolic, Christ Apostolic Church, Faith Tabernacle, Musama Christo Disco, Divine Prayer Society, Cherubim and Seraphim, Celestial Church of Christ, the Brotherhood of the Cross and the Star and the Prophet Harris group. According to Daneel, some prophetic movements specifically do not want to be considered Zionist[19]. A prominent example is the Apostle Church of Johane Maranke, who claims to represent a more authentic version of Christianity than the Zionist churches. They also claim that their doctrine and worship are living examples of the first Apostles of Jesus Christ.[20] Their voice is difficult to ignore because they represent a significant number in Southern Africa: being the largest Indigenous church in Zimbabwe with branches in Zambia, Zaire and Malawi. Turner believes that the diversity of accents in the work of the Holy Spirit justifies a subdivision into soteriological (salvation) and revelational churches.[21]

The soteriological churches place the main emphasis on prophetically guided faith healing.[22] Redemption is interpreted mainly as deliverance from disease caused by demonic forces—especially witches, wizards and evil spirits. Because of the persistent emphasis on healing one could also refer to them as "therapeutic churches."[23] By contrast the "revelational churches" place the emphasis

---

19 Daneel, M.L., *Quest for Belonging*, p40

20 Daneel, M.L., *Zionism and faith-healing in Rhodesia*, The Hague, 1970, p350

21 Turner, H W, *A typology for African religious movements,* in Journal of Religion in Africa, (1)1, 1967 (c), p76

22 Ibid

23 Ibid p77

on revelations given to prophets through the inspiration of the Holy Spirit. In this way, the Spirit regulates church activities and the lives of individual members. 'There are shifts of emphasis, but these are mainly among different congregations of the same church, depending on the tastes and talents of the prophets concerned.'[24] This kind of shift also relates to the Aladura churches in West Africa.

In the opinion of the author, Turner's preference of 'prophet-healing churches' is more applicable to revelational churches. Peel quoted a leader of one of these churches who wrote scathingly about Joseph Babalola, founder of CAC, one of the most powerful prophets, as joining one of the *'churches mighty in prayer but weak in Scripture.*[25] Peel's assessment of being mighty in prayer is the very essence of healing backed by prophetic visions and revelations, through the inspiration of the Holy Spirit. His assessment of being weak in Scripture, is now an anachronism even before the turn of the twentieth century. With the emergence of intellectuals including outstanding academics, professionals, business gurus and theologians in the membership of the Christ Apostolic Church, Cherubim & Seraphim Church and other Aladura groups in Nigeria, Musama Disco Christo Church and Divine Prayer Society in Ghana and elsewhere, the AIC can now rightly claim ascendancy into theological maturity. There is now established, Joseph Ayo Babalola University manned by eminent theologians from within the CAC in Nigeria. Other Aladura groups like Cherubim & Seraphim and Celestial Church of Christ have also started building their own Universities. There are similar

---

24 Daneel, M.L., *Quest for Belonging*, p40

25 Peel, J D Y, Aladura*: A Religious Movement Among the Yoruba*, London, OUP, 1968, P138

initiatives in other parts of Africa where seminaries and colleges of higher education have opened the gateway to the training of AIC ministers and church workers.

Messianic Churches

The term 'Messianic' is basically a sub-division of 'Zionist.' It is a term used to describe groups which, centred around a dominant personality, claim for him special powers involving a form of identification with Christ. Hayward argues that 'when this identification with Christ becomes substitution, the group has ... moved outside the sphere of the Christian Church.'[26] Nathaniel Ndiokwere expressed dissatisfaction with this kind of definition and argues that an AIC prophet must necessarily possess special powers, which make him unique in his community. Such a prophet does not, and cannot usurp the identity of Christ who has given him these powers.[27] Because of the uniqueness in spiritual powers, some of them have been accorded names and titles like: Jesus of Achalla, Jesus of Ikot Ekpene, Jesus of Oyingbo, Samuel Mutendi in Zimbabwe, Simon Kinbangu in Congo, Prophet Harris in Ivory Coast. Have they usurped the messiahship of Christ? Messianism is considered a sub-division of Zionism because the so-called Black Messiahs would not personally confess to be comfortable with accepting such roles. Examples of such prominent leaders who deny the acceptance of Messiah as titles are Leader Olumba Olumba Obu of the Brotherhood of the Cross and the Star in Nigeria, Simon Kimbangu of Congo and Isaiah Shembe of South Africa.

---

26 Hayward, V E W, *African Independent Church Movements*, London, Edinburgh House Press, 1963, p71

27 Ndiokwere, Nathaniel, *Prophecy and Revolution,* London, SPCK, 1981, p 9-10

Sundkler initially used mediation at the gates of heaven as a criterion for a basic distinction of Messianism. The crucial question to be asked is: who stands at the gates of heaven, Jesus Christ or the Black Messiah? If the answer is the latter, then Christ's mediatorship is either violated or superseded and the designation 'Black Messianism' is applicable. Sundkler researched this problem and explained that many Zionist prophetic leaders were attributed with the functions of 'custodian of the heavenly gates' yet this special task was never interpreted in an exclusivist sense as replacing Christ as Mediator.[28] The author finds this explanation satisfactory and there is no sufficient reason for raising the question of substitution.

New Charismatic Churches

These churches adopt some of the characteristics of 'Aladura' theology and modify them with the flamboyance of American preaching, singing and healing styles. Some of them seek to develop what is now popularly known as the 'prosperity gospeling.' An example is the Kingsway Christian Centre operating in East London. This church is reported to be multi-national and commands the largest number of adherents in Europe as a single congregation. The Charismatics operate in similar ways as the Pentecostals. They would not like to be associated with the mainstream AICs and they steer clear of all rituals like the use of water and oil, candles and incense in worship and for prayers. Sundkler's typology predates the emergence of this group. He would have grouped them with the Pentecostals to form a new distinctive group apart from Zionism.

---

28 Daneel, Inus, *Quest for Belonging*, p41

AIC Typology

In Nigeria, there is a group of churches known as 'Winners' They have achieved spectacular growth throughout the country and elsewhere and they are probably the most wealthy of the new AIC's. As they preach 'prosperity gospel' it would be difficult to foresee how long they would remain in popularity. Another new church spreading not only in Nigeria, but also throughout the length and breadth of Africa and other continents is the Redeemed Christian Church of God. Like the Winners, they also preach prosperity gospel but are down to earth in preaching in the fashion of the tele-evangelists. They organise regular conferences for their ministers in order to coordinate their doctrine and to plan missionary strategies for the furtherance of the objectives of their church. They command large followings because their adherents derive more satisfaction in excitement in the youthful exuberance and training of their Pastors. This group will probably like to dissociate themselves from the mainstream AIC, just like the Pentecostals who keep their distance from the Apostolics and the Zionists in Southern Africa.

CHAPTER 3

AIC SWOT ANALYSIS

Notable Strengths

One of the reasons for the emergence of the AIC is the desire to construct a new theology that is relevant to African culture in the first instance, and secondly, to follow certain guidelines which are discernable from the Holy Bible. As a result, to the African thinkers, AIC theology can be appraised as innovative, progressive, bible-based, bible-affirming and bible-fulfilling.[29] It is bible-fulfilling in the sense that signs and wonders are retrieved from obscurity and made realistic in the lives of believers. Hence, it becomes possible to dispense with the services of Traditional healers and to end the ambivalent living of Christians who cannot do without their services. The following exemplify these notions:

Spiritual Renewals

Jesus has always taught by example. He was fond of prayers to the Father. His prayer retreats usually took place at the Mountain, the Wilderness or the Seaside. Many of the AIC have taken to this habit because in these places, one is cut off from the environment which is full of sin. In these places, fuller awareness of the glory of God is bestowed and the devout Christian can be best placed to draw spiritual

---

29 Omoyajowo, J Akindele, op cit, *Cherubim and Seraphim, The History of an African Independent Church,* New York, London, Lagos, Enugu, NOK Publishers International, 1982, p91

strength. Experiences derived from visiting these resorts are similar to the experience of the three Apostles on the Mount of Transfiguration, where Moses and Elijah appeared with Jesus. It is common that some members are baptised with the Holy Spirit for the first time in these places. This is the reason why one will find the AIC making regular pilgrimages to such resorts for spiritual renewal. During the retreats, signs and wonders are very common and many people try to create time to attend for this purpose. In Nigeria, the Cherubim & Seraphim Movement Church has such a retreat in Kaduna, called Mount Horeb, relocated to somewhere else in South West Nigeria called 'Galilee' in Orile Igbon, between Ilorin and Ogbomosho. Annually, Prophets and Senior Leaders of the Church attend a week of prayer, worship, lecture, seminar and renewal on the mountain. Roswith Gerloff has described how believers encounter that kind of a rapture which takes one beyond one's narrow confines into a new plane of existence, or into the inner court of an awareness of the presence of the Divine, which opens up a new perception of life and self:

> *'Touching and falling, weeping and laughing, dancing and speaking in tongues thus become quite natural vehicles of understanding the world, not only with one's intellect but with one's whole self. The Spirit of Jesus enters the depth of people's lives, falls afresh on them, fills them with power . . . .*[30]

To the AIC milieu, the Kingdom is not yet, and the need for fasting is still appropriate. The African wants to cry to God in the time of crisis, and to expect an answer. Emmanuel Milingo has described the concept of the God of the believer thus:

---

30 Gerloff, Roswith I H, *A Plea for British Black Theologies*, Frankfurt am Main, Peter Lang 1991, p62

'This is the God whom we need in Africa. A God who is a real father, one who cares for his children, protects them, gives them security and is accessible. The God who is said to be in the Holy Heaven, who is at peace with himself and does not care about what is happening among the people on earth, is certainly not an African God.' [31]

Milingo's thoughts describe the basis of the AIC approach to communicating with God in prayers and fasting. Although he is a Catholic bishop, his gifts and theology are basically AIC compatible.

Integrated Worship

In Africa, diversities in language, culture and class can be visible even within small communities. Yet, coherent worship in the AIC is still possible and is well managed according to the nature of the diversity. This differs from the idea of homogeneous unit churches proposed by Donald McGovran[32] from the background of sociology. According to his theory for church growth,

> *'People operate better in social groups more than they do as individuals. A social group may be considered a homogeneous unit. It is comprised of one kind of people. It conditions the individual, it makes up his mind; to some degree it controls him. It gives meaning to his life. Among the many aspects of human society none is more important to church growth than these homogeneous units of mankind.'*

---

31 Milingo, E., *The World in Between, Christian Healing and the Struggle for Spiritual Survival*, London, C Hurst & Co. (Publishers) Ltd, 1984, p75

32 McGavran, D.A., (Ed.) *Church Growth and Christian Mission*, New York, Harper & Row, 1965, p69

This method of church growth takes inculturation too far and creates religious apartheid in which the middle class is separated from the working class; black people from whites; aristocrats from peasants; one linguistic tribe from another one. In larger congregations, it is easier to segregate worshippers according to age or language. Each sub-congregation is led by a worship leader and occasionally, all the sections come together either in an open space or by electronic devices linking them together. The Cherubim & Seraphim Movement Church (Ayo Ni O) in SuruLere, Lagos, Nigeria is an example of this kind of structure. They have several kinds of congregations in the same compound: Adult (Yoruba) congregation, English congregation, Youth congregation and a separate congregation for Children. At a certain point in the Service, all the congregations are linked by Television/Radio for important announcements or pronouncements of blessing. At such times, all matters that concern everybody are dealt with. In smaller congregations, all sections are integrated and participation is shared across the board, men and women, young and old, clergy and laity. In all congregations, integration is always across the board, irrespective of class. It is common, therefore, to find within the ranks of Elders and Clergy, men and women, young and old, academics and professionals, traders and craftsmen. Selection is not always by a particular criteria, but by a combination of spiritually gifted and administratively skilled individuals. This pattern is common among most of the AICs but in the newer groups, especially the charismatics, there is more emphasis on training for ministry where educational background is crucial.

Inculturation

The relationship between the gospel and different cultures remains controversial in contemporary missiology. Lesslie Newbigin has argued that

'The gospel endorses an immensely wide diversity among human cultures, but it does not endorse total relativism. There is good and bad in every culture and there are developments continually going on in every culture which may be either creative or destructive, either in line with the purpose of God as revealed in Christ for all human beings, or else out of that line. The criteria for making judgments between one and the other cannot arise from one culture. That is the familiar error of cultural imperialism.'[33]

Conversion of a person requires the conversion of the person on the one hand, and the conversion of his culture on the other. When an individual is converted and not the culture, the result is a partial conversion in which the convert reverts to his culture to find an answer to his problem in the time of crisis. There is certainly a falsity in this dualism and it is necessary to appreciate that 'there is not and cannot be a gospel which is not culturally embodied.'[34] In order therefore, to avoid superficiality in the religion and as a result, living an ambivalent Christian life, full attention must be paid to the culture in which the gospel is preached. Certainly, the Gospel must confront inappropriate aspects of a culture. What it cannot do successfully is to change the culture completely and substitute another strange culture in its place.

Elom Dolvo argues that inculturation is one of the major factors contributing to the growth of AICs. He defined it as a local process of making Christ and the Gospel message of salvation known and understood by people of different cultures, localities and time, using the resources of their culture to promote meaning, acceptance and owning the Gospel. He contends that:

---

33 ,Newbigin, Lesslie, *The Gospel in a Pluralist Society*,London, SPCK, 1992, p197

34 Ibid, p189

'Inculturation in Africa strips the Christian faith of some of its missionary (Western) cultural context in exchange for African cultural idioms that make it relevant and ingrained in its new context.[35]

Elom's description means that Africa can now put a round peg into a round hole. Previously, it was a square peg in a round hole which left gaps. Inculturation is the means by which the gaps can be filled in any cultural setting. In the Nigerian Yoruba traditional religion, there are many gods representing different functions of the life of the people. But there is also a pre-eminent god called 'Olodumare.' Bolaji Idowu explains that the Yoruba people see the god, Olodumare as equivalent to the Christian God.[36] This is because the functions of Olodumare and the Christian God are similar. Substituting the former for the latter posed no problems. It was just a matter of changing names. Hence in all Yoruba Christian liturgy, 'Olodumare' becomes synonymous with 'Almighty.' The Yoruba Bible actually translated 'Almighty' to mean 'Olodumare' It should be recognized that 'Olodumare' is the highest in power and might among all the lesser Yoruba deities. The actual translation should have been 'Alagbara' meaning the one with unlimited power and authority. Some sceptics may call this sacrilege, but the author calls it inculturation. Donal Dorr[37] has explained that there are many similarities between the Yoruba divinities and those of ancient Celtic peoples. He outlined different parallels including the goddess Brighid. He explained:

---

35 Dolvo, Elom, *Exchange, Journal of Missiological and Ecumenical Research, vol 33 No1(2004),* p29

36 Idowu, Bolaji, *Olodumare: God in Yoruba Belief*, London, Longmans, 1962, pp 32-62

37 Dorr, Donal, *Mission in today's world*, Co Dublin, The Columba Press, 2000, p45

Cherubim & Seraphim Epistemology

'When Ireland became Christianised Saint Brigid, who has the same name, took her place and was given many of her functions.'[38]

The author sees this also as inculturation in the making. Similarly, when the Yoruba became Christianised, the Christian God took over the functions of the 'Olodumare'.

Substitution of consecrated water for traditional herbs and medications is one of the aspects of inculturation and a key factor leading to the sustained growth of the AIC. In the African traditional belief, herbs prescribed by herbalists have spiritual powers to effect healing or to provide a solution to problems. Similarly, some Africans believe that water, when sanctified by a prophet, has been charged with power by the Holy Spirit for the same or better results. This change in the substance of the water is similar to the mediaeval doctrine of 'transubstantiation', by which 'the bread and the wine are transformed (at the level of unseen substance) into the body and blood of Christ in the Eucharist; while retaining their outward appearance.'[39] This explanation is enough to dispel the criticism that the new ritual can be tantamount to traditional rituals or a continuation of them. Within the AIC, contextualisation can find a comfortable home among the Zionist and Messianist cultures. It is partly applicable in Ethiopianism but not at all among the Charismatics. There are numerous Jewish-biblical themes which can be developed to provide effective bridges into African worldviews. It is important to understand African worldviews if theology and indeed, missiology is to be meaningfully

---

[38] O hOgain, Daithi, The *Sacred Isle: Belief and Religion in Pre-Christian Ireland*, Cork, Collins Press, 1999, p112 and 203

[39] Pruitt, Raymond M, *Fundamentals of the faith,* Cleveland, White Wing Publishing 1981, p367

applied to meet the spiritual needs of Africans. Bongani Mazibuko has suggested that

"We need to recover a Christian understanding of the ancestors, and discover creative responses to the practice of ancestral veneration, perhaps by developing a Christology of "Christ our Ancestor" or "Christ the New Adam". In theological terms, whereas in the lineage of the old Adam, all have sinned; in the new Adam, all are made alive to God."[40]

Sound theology should always begin with the aspirations of the people. It should be remembered that all biblical interpretation is done from a specific historical situation. To talk of 'Christ our Ancestor' can be alarming but it should be remembered that Jesus shocked the establishment of his days by befriending everyone, including the destitute and hungry, tax collectors and extortioners, men and women, rich and poor. The author affirms this kind of theology because Jesus related to diversity as a friend of the rich and the poor, the learned and the unlearned, of sinners and the self-righteous. It is difficult to blame God for creating diversity. On the other hand, diversity should be celebrated in unity, love and understanding rather than let it be a basis of disagreement and polarisation.

Perceived Weaknesses

There are now numerous AIC theology colleges and a few universities have either been started or about to be started where academic theology is taught. One big difference with the AIC intellectuals is that the possession of a theological qualification does not necessarily entitle the holder to the leadership hierarchy in the church. Recruitment into the hierarchy has always been by selection either

---

40 Mazibuko, B. A , *Mission is Crossing Barriers* ed. Roswith Gerloff, p221-223 - **7** -

by the Holy Spirit through visible evidence of charismatic gifts or by church elders through demonstration of special skills relevant to church ministry. This does not mean that theological skills are not required. Such skills are always channelled to training, teaching, counselling and where the holder is also blessed with charismatic gifts, then ascendancy into the church hierarchy. There are other perceived weaknesses but it will suffice for the purpose of this book to discuss polygamy, ancestor worship, pro Old Testament tendencies, schism and paganism.

Polygamy

First and foremost, it should be understood that the author is a happily married man and does not condone polygamy. His problem lies simply in joining the bandwagon of those who condemn polygamy as being non-Christian. It cannot be denied that the Bible does not specifically condemn polygamy in any of the books. The Ten Commandments does not include 'Thou shalt not marry more than one wife.' It can even be argued that the first century church was built on a culture of polygamy. If that was not the case, Paul would not have had the problem of differentiating between polygamy and monogamy in his letters to Timothy and Titus. Being a celibate minister himself, he recommended celibate ministry for priests, but made the concession of marriage for the weaker ones who could not stand the demands of celibacy, especially for bishops who must in any case be 'the husband of one wife.' He did not condemn polygamy as non Christian. It can be rightly assumed that Paul recognised that a polygamist cannot offer sufficient attention to efficient ministry. He most probably felt that polygamy should be confined to the laity and that the ministry should be limited to those who can give the right level of commitment 'for the perfecting of the saints, for the work of the ministry, for the edifying of the body of Christ.' (Eph. 4:12)

Polygamy is not necessarily evil or ungodly, but it can always be a multiplier of problems in a polygamous family and it can always generate jealousy and animosity in the family. Empirical evidence has shown that problems emanating from polygamy can be managed in a few cases but in most cases, competition, jealousy, strife and even war among siblings have shown why polygamy should be avoided where it is possible. On the negative argument, it can always pose obstacles towards ideal practice of peaceful religion and purity of Christian ethics. Apart from the obscure argument that our patriarchs, Abraham, Isaac and Jacob were polygamists per se, and that God loves them and is always proud of them, Christians and even non Christians should for the sake of peace of mind, steer clear of polygamy.

The question of the relation between the gospel and the different human cultures is one of the most vigorously debated topics in contemporary missiology. There are questions in African culture that can be cited. Polygamy is a thorny issue in African Christianity. Most critics have asserted that Africans cannot be Christians when they encourage polygamy. They imply that monogamy is Christian as if it is expressly written in the Bible. The author confronted respondents to the questionnaire about this issue and there seems to be consensus between AIC and non-AIC respondents. First, it was agreed that the Bible does not expressly condemn polygamy as such but encourages Christians, especially those aspiring to leadership positions, to be either celibate or be the husband of only one wife (I Tim 3).[41].

---

41 Some non-AIC respondents argue that I Tim 3 is not necessarily restricted to leadership but applicable to all Christians, quoting other supporting scriptures. On the other hand, some AIC respondents argue that if monogamy was a blanket criteria for Christianity, why did Paul have to remind Timothy at all?

Cherubim & Seraphim Epistemology

The author is personally convinced that God is neither interested in polygamy nor in monogamy because

in the resurrection they neither marry, nor are given in marriage, but are as the angels of God in heaven.' (Matt. 22:30).

It is therefore erroneous on the part of missionaries to insist that newly converted polygamists should put away all but the first wife. Putting away of wives and retaining only one cannot be seen as an act of kindness and piety as preached in the Gospels. On the contrary, it can be seen as an act of wickedness and contrary to the teaching of Christ. Moreover, it can be argued from the AIC perspective that most of the founding prophets were polygamists and they did not put away any of their wives in order to do their mission. The question arises then whether the Holy Spirit made mistakes in calling the wrong persons to service or that they were never called at all. Newbigin was right to argue that

> *'to contemporary African Christians, looking at Western society with its serial polygamy, it seems obvious that the traditional African pattern is more true to the gospel, since it at least acknowledges binding covenant obligations while the Western model dissolves them.'[42]*

One of the AIC respondents explained that the question of marriage should be separated from the question of personal sanctity[43]. There is a variety of orientation found among the founding prophets of the AIC. Some have been single and celibate like Moses Orimolade of the Cherubim and Seraphim Church; monogamists like Simon Kimbangu in Congo; and polygamists like Joseph Oshofa in

---

42 Newbigin, Lesslie, *The Gospel in a Pluralist Society*, p187

43 Osun, Chris, *Encountering Aladura Spirituality in Britain*, p9

Nigeria and Shembe in South Africa. It is believed that all were sanctified by their calling, and in commonality, signs and wonders were their hallmarks. Therefore, readers should be reminded that *'what God hath cleansed, that call not thou common.' (Acts 10:15)* It is undeniable that monogamy is embedded in Western culture and that polygamy is also embedded in African (and Semitic) culture. However, to imply that because Christian mission proceeded from Europe to Africa, and therefore the latter must adhere to the former's culture, is to deny the universality of the spirit of Pentecost where numerous cultures were represented and heard the good news preached in their own languages, and not just in Hebrew. Asked whether he believes that Christianity should absorb polygamy in Africa, one respondent replied that the church should not condemn those who are already polygamists, but that those who are married to one wife should remain the husband of one wife; and those who are still single and who are already Christians should be encouraged either to remain celibate or marry only one wife.

Paul did not attempt to change round the beliefs of the men at Athens who worshipped the unknown God. He simply introduced Christianity as the true substitute, and from then, Christianity was adopted in the place of the unknown God. Speaking of the doctrine of election, Lesslie Newbigin asked

> *'Would this mean, then, that Hebrew culture has to become the world's culture? Is this, in fact, just one more version of the familiar imperial story, the conviction of one human culture that is the way for all? That is, indeed, what is explicit in the universal claim of Islam. God's will as it is communicated in the untranslatable Arabic of the Qur'an is that to which every human society must conform. There can be no translation.'*[44]

---

44 Newbigin, Lesslie, *The Gospel in a plural society*, SPCK, 1989, p145

Within the AIC, monogamy is considered a Western rather than a biblical culture. Acceptance of polygamy in no way condones immorality in the sense of permissive or loose living, but is subject to moral norms and church control that are strictly enforced. If Christian mission must differ from the Islamic stance, then inculturation should be encouraged in order to allow the mission to cross cultural barriers 'unto the uttermost parts of the world.' That being the case, care should be exercised in the process of inculturation. There can be certain features of African culture which the Gospel should confront assertively. There has been recent publicity of certain African churches involved in excessive exorcism leading to physical abuse of children[45] and another involving trafficking African children into the country[46]. These incidents are certainly isolated cases and not stereotypical across the AIC. They should not be allowed to deter the AIC operators globally in working towards the achievement of their missionary objectives.

Ancestor worship

Another thorny issue which is pertinent to the AIC is the question of ancestor worship. This is found across Africa but is more pertinent to Southern African cosmology. Nevertheless, it is wrong to speak bluntly of ancestor worship by Africans as if it forms a significant aspect of their theology. They do not worship ancestors but see them as living spirits who, although physically dead, but still care for their community spiritually. It should be remembered that a Christian believer does not die.

---

45 Vikram Dodd, *More children 'victims of cruel exorcisms',* The Guardian Saturday Jun 4, 2005, p10

46 Okutubo, 'Femi, Re *Gilbert Deya's 'miracle' babies*, The Trumpet, Vol. 10 No15 Sep. 1-14, 2004,p2

'whosoever believeth in him should not perish, but have everlasting life' (John 3:16).

What is called ancestor worship is nothing more than according the ancestors the status of some kind of mediators. This should not be confused with Jesus as mediator. It is similar to the Roman Catholics praying through certain saints or through Holy Mary as intercessors. Milingo finds in the person of Jesus the link through which this African spirituality can be transformed into a Christian spirituality. Jesus fills for all humanity the role of a supreme ancestor. He sees this as a very noble title, because

> 'when we consider Jesus as an ancestor, it means that he is to us an elder in the community, an intercessor between God (Mwari, the high god) and our community, and the possessor of ethereal powers which enable Him to commune with the world above and with the earth. He is able to be a citizen of both worlds.'[47]

Here, Milingo adopts the principle of substitution or inculturation as exemplified above on the question of marriage. In effect, Milingo does not advocate praying to ancestors, but he finds no fault in cherishing their memory; for although dead, they still remain part of the family life in absentia. Outside of Africa and even in Europe, do people not go to the graveyards and tidy up the graves? put some flowers and stay for some time there?; and even sometimes, do not some visitors to their ancestors' graves speak to the emptiness of the grave as if someone is living there? The only difference here is that the African brings his holistic living to his religion in a different way than to others, who live their lives devoid from any attachment or memory of their ancestors.

---

47 Milingo, E, *The World in Between*, C Hurst & Co. (Publishers) Ltd, 1984, p78

The typical African lives a societal life. He does not exist on his own but in bond with the community, with the ancestors and even with the generation yet unborn. In life or in death, the bond is never broken. This is the one thing which colonisation and Christianity have never succeeded in suppressing. The intensity of maintaining this bond differs from tribe to tribe in Africa. Features of this bond are quite visible till today in churches, not only of the AIC group, but also among the mainline mission churches. One should observe the rituals[48] in naming, marriage and funeral ceremonies in all the churches, and even in social functions in Africa, to have a greater understanding of African spirituality.

The Zionists in Southern Africa today have dissociated themselves from ancestor worship. Pretorius has confirmed that 'Zionists no longer accept that ancestors affect their lives in a dominant way. A female member says with great sincerity and firmness:

"I do not believe in them, I don't put my hope on them as they have no influence over our lives." Another agrees: *"A person serves Christ or the ancestors, not both. We now have Jesus and we have abandoned the habit of attending to the ancestors"*[49]

Nevertheless, it still cannot be said categorically that Africans have completely abandoned their ancestors as evidence shows some continuity in contact through dreams. Most of the Zionists will now choose to ignore such dreams or counter them with prayers.[50] It cannot be ruled out that the bond to the ancestors

---

48 Ibid p76

49 Pretorius, H L, *Ethiopia stretches out her hands unto God,* ISWEN, Pretoria, University of Pretoria, 1993, p99

50 Ibid p100

could eventually be broken in part or completely, depending on developments in ongoing dialogue on the Gospel and culture in the future.

Pro Old Testament

The Old Testament is central to the initiation, development and growth of the AICs, but without neglecting the New. This is because the AICs make extensive use of the Old Testament scripture especially in prayers. There is no good reason in defending the leaning on the Old Testament because Jesus did not come to destroy the Law or the Prophets, but to fulfil. The views of one respondent, who is a Baptist Pastor and Lecturer, and also a co-author of a book on AIC, Dr Deji Ayegboyin[51] represents those who still think that the AICs misuse the Psalms in prayers. Such a Psalm as 35, which is full of curses for the destruction of the enemy is an example cited. The author's answer is that Jesus teaches us to pray for our enemies. If anyone will choose not to bless but to curse, it will be a matter of personal choice and the sinner cannot go unpunished. The important thing to remember is that man can only pray, but the answer comes from God. It is inconceivable to assume that man can issue instruction to God to destroy His own creation! There is simply no logic but foolishness in praying for the enemy's destruction to Him who asks you to bless your enemy. As we pour out our desires in prayer, we should also remember that Jesus is the author and finisher of our faith. Perhaps some may prefer to curse their enemies within the AIC, but their actions do not represent the policy of the whole, and no inference can be made to any faulty approach to African Christianity on this account.

---

51 Ayegboyin, Deji & Ishola, S Ademola, *African Indigenous Churches*, Lagos, Greater Heights Publications, 1997, p87

Because the Bible was translated, Africans could read in their own language and better understand the Scripture. It was like another Pentecost as each Jewish tribe could understand and draw parallels between the Gospel message and their culture. The AICs embrace elements of worshipping God as they see them in the Bible. Some of these elements are familiar out of African religion, but others are new and enriching. The narratives of dreams, visions and prophecy in the Old Testament which resonate with the African culture are not so prominent in the New Testament. Although the latter is full of signs and wonders in its narratives, the former contains powerful stories of anointed leaders and prophets like Moses, Joshua, the twelve Judges, Elijah, Elisha, the Wisdom Literature, and many more useful scripture for preaching and edification. Jesus associated himself with the Old Testament when on the mount of configuration, he appeared with Moses and Elijah. How can all these be thrown away and Christianity limited to the New Testament?

The healing ministry is the most common feature of the AICs. In this practice, the Old Testament is used more than the New. It is the practice that Scriptures are read with prayers for motivation and affirmation. This can happen in two ways. Either that the scripture reading is given through vision or prophecy; or that the leader of service uses his/her discretion to prescribe the scripture. In both cases, the book of Psalms is extensively used because it is full of songs of praise and prayers for different purposes. The Prophets, especially Isaiah and Ezekiel are also frequently used. Others include I /II Kings and Exodus. In the New Testament, the healing miracles of Jesus in the Gospels, a few healing prayers of Peter and Paul in Acts and James chapter five are frequently used for healing prayers.

Old Testament Taboos

There are many practices derived from the Old Testament which are found within the AICs. Some do not wear shoes in worship because they believe that the worship area of the church should be holy to the Lord. This derives from the burning bush experience of Moses (Exodus 3:5) and particularly that God personally voiced the command to Moses. Joshua also had similar experience at Jericho when the captain of the Lord's host commanded him to 'loose thy shoe from off thy foot; for the place whereon thou standest is holy.' The AICs in this tradition of worshipping barefooted are: in Southern Africa, the Zion Church of Christ; in West Africa, the Cherubim and Seraphim Church, the Celestial Church of Christ, the Church of the Lord Aladura, the Brotherhood of the Cross and the Star. These churches also encourage every member to robe in white during worship.

For the same reason of holiness, these same churches observe the strict hygienic rites of Leviticus. All things considered as an abomination to the Lord are not allowed into the Prayer House. Blood is one main example. Women in their menstruation period are barred until they are clean again. Wounded people still covered in blood or people who have touched blood, or have shed blood, irrespective of sex, are also barred. It is believed that for this reason amongst others, God disallowed David as a soldier, to build the Temple for Him, and instead, gave the honour to his son, Solomon. Other abominations barred from the Prayer House include dead bodies. Funeral services are conducted in the premises of the deceased instead of the Prayer House, and internment at the graveside, the same way as other churches. It is claimed in defence of this that God is not the God of the dead, but of the living (Lk 20:38).

There are rules of certain AICs relating to food consumption. In Southern Africa, the Zion Church of Christ forbids the eating of meat of animals killed by violence and accident because their blood would not be completely drained from their bodies. (in Nigeria, the Yoruba call such meat as 'eran igbe') Hence African hunters who go to the bush to shoot down animals; and those who set traps to catch animals to be marketed in the shops, will not find customers amongst the Zionists. Meat eaten by them should be systematically and ritually slaughtered. Among the West African Aladuras, the ritual for slaughtering animals and fowls for domestic consumption would take the form of a short prayer like: 'Cursed be to the name of Satan; glory be to the name of the Lord.' After this, the knife is struck into the neck of the victim and the head is held tightly until the last drop of blood and until there is no longer movement from the animal. This is similar to the Jewish practice and also the Muslim belief in 'halal meat' consumption. Nevertheless, even among those AICs whose doctrine does not place restrictions on food consumption, there are still certain people who are restricted by divine command through dreams, visions and prophecies to abstain from eating meat.

Schism

Schism is defined in Oxford Illustrated Dictionary as 'breach of unity of a Church, separation into two Churches or secession of part of Church owing to difference of opinion on doctrine or discipline.' It is a fact that schism is very rampant within the AIC. Researchers have produced statistics of AIC churches numbering thousands of small denominations across Africa and that the trend continues. David Barrett[52] lists as many as six thousand

---

52 Barrett, David, in *Schism and Renewal in Modern Africa,* Nairobi, OUP, 1968, P57

separatist religious movements and groupings in Africa. This statistics affirms the fact that one of the most unseemly aspects of the AICs is their tendency to fragment continually into a multiplicity of autonomous groups and denominations. This can be described as un-Christian not only because there is strength in unity, but also because Jesus particularly prayed for unity of his followers before his ascension. Schism can arise out of disagreement with certain aspects of a doctrine. For instance, the method of baptism is controversial and some Christians believe it should be a sacrament for adult believers on the one hand and that it should be by immersion on the other.

Some believe in the Matthew 28 formula of the Trinity, and some in the Apostolic formula of simply 'in the name of the Lord', as in Acts 2. Even among the Trinitarians who do immersion, some believe that the immersion should be once, and others, thrice. Such little differences in doctrine can always cause division leading to schism. Another possible cause is on the ground of nationalism. This is common among the 'Ethiopian' churches. They separate from their church in order to be free to dominate church polity which would allow for ease of contextualisation of certain aspirations of their culture. Some schism among the AICs emanates from unhealthy rivalry among ambitious aspirants to high office in the church. When an aspirant cannot have his way, the result is always separation. This is common especially where an outgoing leader leaves his succession open. When a leader fails to groom a capable successor, his own success in office can become a failure as he leaves chaos behind him. Other sources of schism will include incompatibility between, for instance, a minister and his church wardens or other officers. If frequent disagreement becomes the order of the day for them, such a church could be heading towards schism.

Schism is one thing Africans have copied badly from Europeans who brought Christianity in a number of denominational bodies. The pity is that what Africans copy, they tend to go the extra mile. This habit is clearly discernible in the current wave of abuse of power and corrupt practices which are rampant within the commercial and political life in Africa. Schism is bad enough for copying but perhaps inevitable, considering the environment in which the AICs have developed and grown. There is no advantage of strong central controlling bodies for most of the AICs. As a result, people do go down the road casually to start their own church under a different name as soon as there is an unresolved dispute. Perhaps the AIC must necessarily go through these teething problems before the emergence of a more credible profile towards the advancement of the gospel and the preparation for the Lord's parousia. For the AICs to minimise the incidence of schism, there must be established strong central controlling bodies to regulate the activities of ministers and their church workers. A recognised head or executive must be vested with enough powers to mobilise the resources of the church in personnel, property and finance. Most of the AICs are not yet on that road.

Paganism

At the very beginning, the theology of the AIC was difficult to understand. The fact that mainline churches and scholars saw the new movement as deviant from the norm, the norm being the way the missionaries to Africa taught Christianity there; coupled with the fact that these new churches in their opinion were unlicensed and unauthorised, complicated the problem and resulted in condemnation of the AICs. Sundkler, in his first edition of 'Bantu Prophets in South Africa', saw the churches as *a 'bridge over which Africans are brought back to the old heathenism from whence they once came.'*[53]

But in the second edition, (1961), after many years of research and interaction with the AIC, Sundkler saw more light and the error of his initial judgement, repented and modified his stance:

> *'To the African masses . . . .their churches appeared as definitely Christian organisations, adapted to their own real needs, and as bridges to a new and richer experience of life. In the city, with its rapidly industrialised civilization, they functioned as 'adaptive structures'. In Zululand and Swaziland they were, relatively speaking, reaching the difficult transition period from traditional religion to new structures and a new ideology'* [54]

This notwithstanding, some critics like Beyerhaus, as mentioned below, still think that the paganism stigma should remain on the AICs. They have welcomed Christianity wholeheartedly and have totally forsaken traditional religion. But in the process, the AICs have intensified rituals in the use of consecrated water and oil primarily for healing and also for seeking solution to other adversities. Most AICs light white candles and flick incense in worship and during prayers. These practices have been offensive to other Christians, especially the Pentecostals who associate such rituals to pagan worship. But these rituals also feature in the worship of the Catholics and the Anglican high church. The substitution of rituals in worship is the equivalence of what an African will miss from the traditional religion. As long as Jesus is at the centre

---

53 Sundkler, Bengt, *Bantu Prophets in South Africa*, Pretoria, Lutterworth Press, 1948, p55

54 Sundkler Bengt , *Bantu Prophets of South Africa*, Lutterworth Press, Pretoria, 1961, p302

of the rituals, the AIC should be seen to be on the right side of Christianity.

Despite their effort to sever the African people from traditional religion, the AIC have not totally escaped the criticism of scholars. Oosthuizen, Marie-Louise Martin and Beyerhaus who have all adopted a condemnatory approach.[55] Oosthuizen bluntly refers to the AIC as 'post-Christian', In his view,

'these movements are neither Christian nor traditional. Because of their ethnocentric features they cannot claim to be churches of Christ.' [56]

Oosthuizen is entitled to his own opinion but nevertheless, the majority of scholars today accept that the AIC effectively represents a significant opinion in African Christianity which will continue to play a leading role in Christian mission and evangelism not only in Africa, but also globally in the not distant future.

---

55 Daneel, Inus, *Quest for Belonging*, p246

56 Oosthuizen, G.C., *Post-Christianity in Africa—A theological and anthropological study*, London, C Hurst & Co, 1968

CHAPTER 4

BACK TO BASICS

In the Cherubim & Seraphim liturgy for Divine Worship, we very often include 'Prayers for Spiritual Gifts for All Members'. This request frankly means that all members are required to be taken from ordinary to extraordinary; from lower level to higher level in all ramifications of life; from natural results to supernatural results. It is a quest for restoring thaumaturgy and ethereal gifts that were so common in first century Christianity. Those gifts are divine and fundamental to effective adoration and worship of the most high God. That is why they were included in the package of the gifts that descended on the day of Pentecost to equip the saints for the smooth running of the church as driven by the Holy Spirit.

Undoubtedly, Christianity today, especially among the mainline older denominations has drifted far away from the original culture of the first century Christians as narrated in the New Testament.

- The business of the church then was inspired for Kingdom exploits, and Holy Spirit driven. Thaumaturgy and ethereal gifts were common features of church life.

- Signs and wonders were the hallmarks of the church and evangelism was at its highest peak.

- Spirituality took precedence over secular priorities and vanity of life.

- Religion and Politics were acknowledged as opposing forces and there was clear demarcation between 'what belongs to

Caesar' on the one hand, and 'what belongs to God' on the other.

- The commandments of God were taken seriously, and as opposed to the present practice, the Sabbath was observed and taken as sacred.

- The Fifth Commandment asking for generational respect for elders, and by implication, higher authorities, were taken seriously and observed.

- There was serious belief in, and earnest hope for the Rapture of Christ as it was specifically hinted in the Gospels and in the apocalypse Scripture.

The enthusiasm as outlined above, inter alia, did not last long and affinity with and interaction with politics cum secularism became prominent in the lives of Christians. The church seems to have lost its saltiness; as the role of the Holy Spirit became relegated from primary to secondary status.

Informed academic theologians and missionaries have become convinced that the ethereal Pentecostal powers of the first Apostles have disappeared with their exit from life and ministry. Faith, which was the raison d'etre on which signs and wonders were anchored gradually faded away. Any mention of supernatural powers now becomes scary, suspicious and branded as almost, if not absolutely paganistic and unchristian. Practical Christianity with its ethereal dynamics has now been perceived as an anachronism.

Apostolic succession in the church has become less and less effective and the profile of the first Apostles has become like fables and no longer relevant. The healing of the lame man at the Beautiful Gate by Peter and John now has become a distant past that cannot be repeated. The succession process is supposed to carry with it both temporal and spiritual dynamics. Whilst the temporal is now laboriously celebrated, the ethereal dynamics seem to be no longer practicable nor relevant; and therefore locked up in some archaic and dormant storage room.

The church, especially in Europe has compromised with secular priorities and indeed has become nothing more than a Servant to the State. The seed of spirituality seemed to have drifted from fertile grounds and has become entangled in hostile and thorny environments where it could no longer grow naturally, but frustrated into dysfunctionalism. Jesus gave a warning in His Sermon on the mount:

Ye are the salt of the earth: but if the salt have lost his savour, wherewith shall it be salted? It is thenceforth good for nothing, but to be cast out, and be trodden under foot of men. Ye are the light of the world. A city that is set on a hill cannot be hid. Neither do men light a candle, and put it under a bushel, but on a candlestick; and it giveth light unto all that are in the house. Let your light so shine before men, that they may see your good works, and glorify your Father which is in heaven.(Matt.5:13-16).

This sermon requirement is precisely where the church is expected to position itself. It is not supposed to be easy and convenient to maintain the 'saltiness' and to provide the 'light' to lighten the darkness of the world. The church has wrongly taken solace in Paul's comments on ethereal dynamics in I Corinthians 13:1-3:

Though I speak with the tongues of men and of angels, and have not charity, I am become as sounding brass, or a tinkling cymbal. And though I have the gift of prophecy, and understand all mysteries, and all knowledge; and though I have all faith, so that I could remove mountains, and have not charity, I am nothing.

In this narrative, I believe that Paul was only warning the Corinthians against arrogance in thinking of themselves more highly than they ought to; because of their new found talents. The reality is that the church has, because of this, degenerated gradually into a more convenient and comfortable zone where little or no effort is required to keep the spiritual flame burning. It is quite possible to exercise these ethereal gifts and yet be humble. Apparently, the Corinthians to whom Paul wrote did not grasp the need for, and the virtue of humility in ministry and so became arrogant. What they needed was more tutoring and mentoring to correct; and less of rebuke and discouragement which can lead to quenching of the spirit and to slumberness.

But the church owes it to God to work hard and prevail against slumberness and to keep the flame burning. The door to regain supernatural powers is never closed but it requires great efforts and sacrifice to retrieve the lost ethereal dynamics. Moses could not prevail against Amalek when he let down his hands.

But Moses' hands were heavy; and they took a stone, and put it under him, and he sat thereon; and Aaron and Hur stayed up his hands, the one on the one side, and the other on the other side; and his hands were steady until the going down of the sun. And Joshua discomfited Amalek and his people with the edge of the sword (Ex 17:13/14)

The effort of Moses in ensuring victory to Joshua and his soldiers over Amalek was not cheap and easy. It required great effort and agony for him to spend hours standing on top of the hill holding his hands high with the assistance of his aids. Only if the church could sacrifice more energy and resources, coupled with strong faith in God's mercy and providence than presently done, would signs and wonders return to believers. In fighting a battle or war to victory, God could deliver victory with very little or no effort on the part of the Israeli soldiers. But on this occasion, God required concerted effort and sacrifice from the Israeli leadership. Moses and his aides stood up to the challenge faithfully before victory was delivered.

God works in mysterious ways in order to perform His wonders. Moses was praying on the hill and Joshua was in the battle field, fighting against Amalek. This episode is similar to what happened to Peter in the prison. His deliverance to freedom came as a result of prayers by the faithful on his behalf (Acts 12:5).

When they were past the first and second ward, they came unto the iron gate that leadeth unto the city; **which opened to them of his own accord;** *and they went out, and passed on through one street; and forthwith the angel departed from him. (Acts 12:10)*

When Philip finished the assignment of baptising the Ethiopian Eunuch in the desert, he **disappeared and was later found preaching in different cities and locations**.

(Acts 8:39-40). How did it happen? many would begin to wonder, Several times, Jesus appeared to, and disappeared from his disciples in a way they could not understand. They only recognised Jesus when he repeated his usual acts like blessing meals and inviting them to the table or simply saying 'fear not' or 'peace be with you'. No questions were asked. The disciples were only amazed and delighted. They did not understand how and why such feats happened but later, Philip re-enacted the act in the desert. Moses Orimolade performed similar feats as he crossed rivers without the ability to swim; and also travelled up and down a vast country like

Nigeria for about seven years in his itinerary mission, again mostly on foot as motorised vehicles were scarce in Nigeria at his time.

These kinds of signs and wonders are very common in both Old and New Testaments but presently, they have been written into history. But despite our shortcomings, God has not finished with His church yet. It would appear that the Holy Spirit sought new pastures and found fertile grounds elsewhere from time to time and from place to place. Through Revivals and the emergence of Pentecostalism, the Holy Spirit has put a new song back into Christianity: The song in Amazing Grace goes:

'Once I was lost, but now I'm found.'

(The saltiness that was lost has now been restored);

'was blind, but now I see.'

(The light that was mistakenly placed under a bushel has now been correctly placed on it and many can now see).

The restoration and the correction are the dynamics of Revivals and Pentecostalism that emerged during the last two centuries.

During the late 19th and early 20th centuries, the condition of the church of Christ which had degenerated to a state of repair over the centuries suddenly found the Holy Spirit moving across the continents, from South America, North America, Africa, Asia and Europe. Pentecostal revivals took place in several locations, some receiving publicity and some without; due to obscurity of locations and literacy differentials. Scanning these revivals from the most popular to the most obscure, we have the Azusa Street Revival in 1906 which has since become popularly labelled as the 'mother of all revivals' and giving birth to modern Pentecostalism. Similarly, other revivals took root in other parts of the world during the same period. Among these were, inter alia:

- 1904 South Wales in Britain led by Evan Roberts
- 1906 Azuza Street, led by William Seymour in Los Angeles, USA
- 1907 Pyongyang in North Korea led by Kil Sun-joo
- 1907 Chile, South America imported from United States
- 1909 South Africa, in Johannesburg, Cape Colony, Dormfontein & Pretoria
- 1916 Christ Army Church of Nigeria founded by Garrick Sokari Braid
- 1918 Precious Stone in Ijebu-Ode, Nigeria; led by Joseph Shadare
- 1921 Congo Revival led by Simon Kimbangu
- 1924 Zion Church of Christ in South Africa led by Engenas Barnabas Lekganyane
- 1925 Cherubim & Seraphim in Lagos, Nigeria led by Moses Orimolade Tunolase
- 1930 Christ Apostolic Church in Nigeria, led by Joseph Babalola
- 1930 Church of the Lord, Aladura in Nigeria, led by Josiah Ositelu

There are other mini Revivals or precursors taking place before the list as above but which did not end up as missions and faded away at the demise of the founding Prophets.

It will suffice to mention just a few to show that the Holy Spirit has not left the church of Christ; and has been busy as ever from time to time, and from place to place. The question may arise as to how it can be ascertained that the above are Holy Spirit motivated. The simple answer is that signs and wonders can be discerned in these movements. Jesus sent a similar answer to John the Baptist in his moments of doubting; and while his expectations were unmet, particularly during his imprisonment. Jesus told his emissaries to draw his attention to the fact that:

'The blind receive their sight, and the lame walk, the lepers are cleansed, and the deaf hear, the dead are raised up, and the poor have the gospel preached to them.' (Matt. 11:6)

Some of the Revivals as above listed I call **'reactionary'** and some, **'organically'** grown. An example of a reactionary Revival is the Braid Movement which began around 1910 in the Niger Delta Pastorate Church, a semi-independent all-African section of the Anglican church, where Garrick Sokari Braid developed special spiritual powers for faith healing and exorcism. His cleansing exploits and preaching led to adherents forsaking idol worshipping and abstinence from drinking alcohol. As a result, idol altars were destroyed and sale of alcohol plummeted with the subsequent dramatic drop in tax revenue from the sale of imported alcohol. In 1916 Braid was arrested and jailed for inciting the community against the State. Despite his arrest and imprisonment, Braid was hailed by his followers as a prophet[57] After his death in 1918 his

---

[57] Ludwig Frieder, *Journal of Religion in Africa*, 23(4) p296-317.

followers established 'Christ Army Church of Nigeria' with Braid as Founder.

Another example of a reactionary Revival is the case of the Precious Stone in Ijebu-Ode, Nigeria. The founders were innocent members of an Anglican Church who were excommunicated as a result of their development of loud and vigorous prayers, speaking in tongues; deliverance and healing practices; events that were alien to the teaching of the missionaries in the Anglican communion. The ex-communicated gladly left their church to form a new group named, 'Precious Stone Society', and later changed to 'The Faith Tabernacle' which was later accredited by the Apostolic Mission from America.

The second group of Revivals were 'organically' grown as the founding Prophets were mysteriously called. An example is Moses Orimolade of the Cherubim & Seraphim from Ikare, Nigeria who was mysteriously conceived, born, and who was not educated but grew up engaging in scholarly dialogue with learned clergy in Sunday School sessions; and performing miracles even from his youth. This mystery is akin to the high level of scriptural knowledge of twelve years old Jesus, displayed in the Temple, and which baffled the learned Scribes and Priests of his day.

Orimolade became an unwanted knowledgeable critic despite his illiteracy. Although he helped to enrich established ministries wherever he went without any ulterior motive, yet he was always rejected and unappreciated by his host ministers. His talents were perceived as more interesting and authentic than that of the hosts ministers, and hence attention of the congregants were diverted to him more than the host ministers. For this reason, he was perceived as a threat by the latter and in order to minimise distraction from their ministries, Orimolade was rejected at each place of ministry.

Cherubim & Seraphim Epistemology

Because of rejection and expulsion from place to place, he inadvertently became an itinerant preacher for about seven years, before he finally arrived in Lagos which led to the subsequent emergence of the church now known as 'Cherubim & Seraphim'.

Apparently, Moses Orimolade started his preaching and healing ministry around the same time as Garrick Sokari Braid. It is possible that both their ministries did overlap. But there is no indication that both were in contact with each other; nor is it clear whether they knew about each other before their deaths.

Preaching the Gospel, conversion from idolatry and baptising people into Christianity, practising faith healing and recruiting adherents for local churches were common to both prophets. Whilst Braid ministered around Opobo, Bonny and Bakana areas of Niger Delta; Orimolade's missionary journey spanned the length and breath of Nigeria; with his itinerary ministry commencing from Ikare in Southwest of Nigeria, upwards to many parts of Northern Nigeria, before returning southward and reaching Lagos in 1924. More will be said about Orimolde in another chapter.

A similar prophet mysteriously called into an 'organic' ministry was Simon Kimbangu of the Belgian Congo. He was a Catechist who turned into a faith healer and was expelled from his church and jailed by the Belgian authorities, charged for inciting people from his community against the authorities, teaching 'false' doctrines and obstructing the flow of trade in alcohol consumption and imported medicines. He died later in prison, though his healing ministry continued after his death. His son was inspired to follow his footsteps as signs and wonders continue to increase in the ministry. After independence, the Kimbangu Church became the largest and also the established church of the country. Elaborate details of this calling and ministry is definitely interesting but is not the subject of this book. It will suffice to touch on the commonalities that can be discerned from these prophets and their ministries. As much as possible, parallels will be drawn between their ministries and Bible narratives.

A Word of Caution

Jesus did warn that at the end time, many antiChrist will emerge to deceive as many saints as they can. This is part of Satan's strategy to maximise his recruitment and to populate hell, where he will eventually end up in destruction by everlasting fire.

For there shall arise false Christs, and false prophets, and shall shew great signs and wonders; insomuch that, if it were possible, they shall deceive the very elect

(Matt. 24:24)

Signs and wonders can abound by Satanic means. Many will be mystified and deceived by them. But one should be careful to look for the end result of such feats. Have the signs resulted in divine deliverance and healing? Have they delivered solution to problems? Are such solutions temporary or permanent? The Bible says, *'by their fruits, ye shall know them' (Matt, 7:20 by)*. Signs and wonders as exhibited by false prophets and pastors can be quite rhetoric and mystifying but in most cases, they show little or no substance. It should be recognised that whenever Jesus healed, the healing was permanent and there was no need for repeat prescription. There have been several 'so called' Crusades where innocent victims fall in spirit at the touching of a false pastor or prophet; but without resulting in solution to their problems! Many people just get carried away simply by what they see, especially from sugar coated tongues of rhetorical imposters. The Bible speaks of such imposters as bound to be told,

'I never knew you. depart from me, ye that work iniquity (Matt. 7: 23). There shall be weeping and gnashing of teeth (Lk 13:28).

Life cycle of the church

The life cycle of the church of Christ has taken a similar pattern to the life cycle of man; from cradle to teenage, to adulthood, old age and death. But it is certain the church will never end up in death nor in extinction; but rather, in Rapture when Christ will come again to reign in the world. Meanwhile, the church is still going through its metamorphosis stage by stage. The future of the church cannot be determined by man. But it is possible to sketch the past to the present. The following is the author's outline of this metamorphosis or its historical stages:

Stage I—The promise of Jesus was fulfilled with the arrival of the Comforter and the birth of the church on the day of Pentecost. Most of the disciples present then received power from on high. Signs and wonders were common occurrences amongst the believers. Baptism of adherents took place from time to time in their thousands at a go, because evangelism and anointing was at its highest.

Stage II—The church started with its expansion from Jewish cultural context to the Gentiles of different cultures. During this stage, the church interacted with strange bedfellows including the State, politics and wealth over many centuries. The combination of these interactions then grew into cancerous infection that resulted in suffocation and loss of its ethereal dynamics. At this stage, the church has become unrecognisable and cannot be reconciled with the church of the first century.

Stage III—is the emergence of Revivals and Pentecostalism. This stage made a bold attempt at restoration of the dynamics and impact of spirituality on believers. Signs and wonders became visible again in the life of the church. But presently especially in the 21st century, the phenomenon looks like waning away in intensity and effectiveness. Prominent among the factors contributing to loss of impact is the distraction of prosperity gospelling. Most of the so-called Pentecostal and other churches today can be described more accurately as 'Business' rather than 'Spiritual' Centres. Emphasis has shifted from spirituality into materialism. Ecclesiastical success is now measured in terms of the number of adherents, in the development of mega congregations and in the size of bank balances.

Stage IV—in the life cycle of the church is the impending doom that seems to be hovering over it. Other religions are combined in conspiracy to mount a deadly assault on Christianity and possibly to wipe it out of existence, as they successfully did in Turkey and North Africa during the past few centuries. The hope for the church now is the prayer that the Master of the sea will hear our despairing cry, and to intercede to lift His church out of the stormy sea and into the next stage, which could be, into safety and expansion, in preparation for His kingdom; or into Rapture when Christ will come again to reign in the world indefinitely; and all the saints will reign with Him in glory.

Even if the belief in the latter is increasingly disappearing especially among academic theologians and unbelieving Christians; but the fact still remains that it was prophesied that

'The grass withereth, the flower fadeth: but the word of our God shall stand for ever' (Isaiah 40:8)

Jesus himself specifically echoes the same:

'Heaven and earth shall pass away: but my words shall not pass away' (Matt.24:35; Lk.21:33).

If Isaiah's prophecy and the affirmation of Jesus are taken as the words of God, then believers should have no good reason to doubt the authenticity of the above narratives. The argument that two thousand years of expectation of fulfilment of the prophecy has not been met does not necessarily invalidate the words of Scripture. A thousand years in the sight of God is like the twinkling of an eye. This is a matter of faith in the word of God and of our Lord Jesus Christ. God is always faithful in His promises. It is always our doubts and shortcomings that seem to negate the words of God.

The Rapture

Like divinity, rapture is not specifically written in the Bible. It is simply a term used to describe the second coming of our Lord Jesus Christ to reign in the world. It is when heaven will come down to the earth, and when there will be transformation everywhere. The usual evils of injustice, intimidation, corruption, undue domination, egoism, nepotism, tribalism, pride, brutality, suppression of the truth, deceit, cheating, looting and the like, will be wiped out and holiness and righteousness will be established by our Christ in His government. Then that part of the Lord's prayer will be fulfilled:

'... *Thy kingdom come, Thy will be done in earth, as it is in heaven*' *(Matt. 6:10)*

Rapture is a beautiful and desirable concept and although its timing is unpredictable, it is as sure as death. It will dawn on us like a thief in the night, when we least expect it. The Gospels told us clearly as outlined above; and it is confirmed by Paul, warning that

In a moment, in the twinkling of an eye, at the last trump: for the trumpet shall sound, and the dead shall be raised incorruptible, and we shall be changed. (I Cor. 15:52).

The concept of the rapture is firmly embedded in the Christian Creeds:

From the commonly used Apostles' Creed:

... And sitteth on the right hand of God the Father Almighty, from thence he shall come to judge the quick and the dead

From the Nicene Creed:

... And sitteth on the right hand of the Father. And shall come again with glory to judge both the quick and the dead; whose kingdom shall have no end.

From the Athanasian Creed:

... is seated at the right hand of the Father, from where he will come to judge the living and the dead ...

Those Christians who have reasons to disbelieve the concept of the Rapture should be advised to discontinue their membership of the Christian denominations in which the Creeds are ceremoniously celebrated in their liturgies, if they would be free from the accusation of false worship. It is worthy of note that it is not all Christian denominations that recite the Creeds in their worship and they are not obliged to. Like the concepts of Trinity and Rapture, the Creeds, although biblically based and spiritually composed, are not specifically written in the bible. They were composed by the church Councils in the early centuries after sufficient dialogue and consensus. It is important to note, therefore, that the Creeds are not the property of any one denomination. It is available for use by all Christian denominations, especially by the Trinitarian Christians who thoroughly understand the wordings and who are totally committed to imbibe the meaning in their daily lives.

Some sceptics have the idea that they were composed by the Roman Catholic Church. Hence, they erroneously change the words 'I believe in the . . . 'holy catholic church . . . ' by substituting the name of their churches for 'holy catholic church' in the belief that 'catholic church' meant 'Roman Catholic Church'. It should be noted that the word 'catholic' in the Creeds means simply, 'universal' or 'global'. Although through human frailty, Christianity is today split into different denominations with different doctrines, but the church is one; or should be one, because Christ is the head of the church (of whatever label) and Christ cannot be divided.

Division or schism is contrary to the plan of God. To rebel and to divide is nothing more than to embrace the wrath of God. He is the only one who can rightly divide because He is Almighty. God divided the nation of Israel into two kingdoms only because of the sins of Solomon, who disobeyed God by worshipping idols of his neighbouring countries. That is why Jesus prayed for his disciples before his ascension into heaven *'that they may be one, as we are' (John 17:11)*. It is needless to affirm that unity is divine, and division is evil. One of the regrets of God is that He created man in His own image. To be perfect, to be obedient and to be Holy, God should have created man without giving him the freedom to choose between good and evil. Because the latter is easier and more convenient, man is more inclined to commit sin than to be obedient to God and His laws.

It is probably blasphemous to say God made mistakes because the creation narratives in Genesis assert that at every stage of creation, God made an inspection and satisfied Himself that 'it was good' If that was the case, why did it start going wrong? Beginning with Adam and Eve in the Garden of Eden and their expulsion due to disobedience; through the attempted correction with the Flood and Noah's Ark; the destruction of Sodom and Gomorrah; the calling of Abraham and the growing of a 'peculiar people, a royal priesthood' in Egypt over four hundred years and the desire to showcase the new creation as examples of obedient people created 'in our own image'. See how these 'peculiar people' misbehaved in the wilderness for over forty years and now rather than behave themselves in the promised land, the 'peculiar people' have not shown sufficient sign of honouring the covenant of God. Looks like the correction exercise will be ongoing until the Rapture; when all anomalies will be terminated and Christ the Lord will reign on earth with His saints indefinitely.

CHAPTER 5

THE MISSION OF CHERUBIM & SERAPHIM CHURCH

The emergence of Cherubim & Seraphim Church (like other AICs) into global Christianity is of divine initiative. It was the answer to the quest for wholesomeness in Christianity, devoid of any association with, or dependence on Traditional Religions and cultural paganism. The missionaries taught adherents to abandon paganism, idol worshipping and to forsake interaction with Traditional Religions, and to cling to Christianity for solution to their problems. Whereas Traditional Religions had invariably provided adequate escape routes to several adversities of the African, the taught missionary models left gaps for a wholesome solution. The implication then meant that the African believers began to live an ambivalent life; worshipping God with all their hearts but resorting to traditional means for solution to their problems in times of crises.

The missionaries came with their teaching of the Bible which did not include teaching on faith and did not provide answers to most problems. Their missions were genuine as they could teach what they knew and believed. But most of the teaching of Jesus in the Gospels have always put emphasis on faith, leading to problem solutions. Jesus very often rebuked his disciples for insufficiency in confidence and faith. Jesus taught that faith was necessary and important to successful ministry, even if it was as small as the mustard seed! It looks like such faith is currently very scarce in the church and has now been replaced with developments in science and technology! The latter emanates from the wisdom of man, whereas religion based on faith for efficacy of prayer is of divine orientation.

The main problem with faith is that it does not work for everyone. Where that is the case after several attempts, the easy and convenient route out of feeling a sense of defeat is to conclude that deliverance and healing based on faith can no longer be relevant to problems of today. It can only belong to the past and to those who still indulge in supernatural powers. Whenever the latter is mentioned today, most Christians become uncomfortable, nervous and suspicious of practising paganism.

It is true that Traditional Religions are basically rooted in supernatural beliefs. It should be understood that such beliefs are not the prerogative of Traditional Religions. Supernatural powers are both positive and negative, holy and unholy. But there will always be a difference. That is why the miracles of Moses in Egypt proved superior to those exhibited by Pharaoh's magicians; why the powers of Elijah baffled the failure of Baal prophets; why the Demoniac spirits recognised Jesus as the son of God who is destined to judge the world at His second coming. The man possessed by multiple spirits cried out to Jesus:

What have I to do with thee, Jesus, thou Son of the most high God? I adjure thee by God, that thou torment me not. (Mk 5:7)

The spirit world which is invisible to humans is inhabited by both holy and unholy spirits. The unholy already know that they would end up in hell when Jesus will come to judge the dead and the living. They are only playing for time, knowing that they are destined for destruction. But before the judgement day, they retain the power to do both good and evil at will. They therefore take the opportunity to deceive as many as possible so as to populate hell; and to deprive God of as many saints as possible from reigning with Christ in His kingdom.

Belief in supernatural powers.

What is supernatural power? Is it real or imaginary? Is it Christian or is it anti-Christ? Is it magic or can any ordinary person acquire the powers? Certainly it is not a common experience. It can be described as extra-ordinary and it requires explanation about its practicality to ordinary people to understand and to appreciate its virtues. Paul, writing to the Ephesians pointed out the need to recognise that as Christians, we should not be fighting

'against flesh and blood, but against principalities, against powers, against the rulers of the darkness of this world, against spiritual wickedness in high places.' (Eph. 6:12)

In essence, Paul recognised the existence of supernatural powers and negative influences that impact on our lives, whether we can see them or not. To deny their existence and influence is to put our lives in danger and unnecessary suffering. We need to recognise them and be ready to fight them but we cannot do the fighting without faith, prayers and fasting. Fighting against principalities and powers cannot be done physically because they are invisible to the naked eye. The war against them must therefore be spiritually executed. How then can anyone fight spiritual war without knowledge of, and interaction with the spiritual world? This knowledge of, and interaction with, is the point of contention between the AICs and other Christian denominations that refuse to have anything to do with it. While the AICs seek to reactivate and to embrace thaumaturgy, non AICs prefer to demonise it.

This is one of the differences between the teaching of the missionaries and African Initiated Churches. The latter has taken initiatives to retrieve and restore the lost virtues and powers of the first century Christianity that makes a difference to the missionaries' model. It is such a difference that provoked the suspicion of non-AIC Christians to suggest that Africans cannot be true Christians as long as they do not comply with Western Christian norms. But critics of the AIC have ignored the very fact that Western Christianity cannot in any way be compared with the First Century Christianity beginning from Jerusalem within the context of Judaism and in the Semitic culture.

Western Christianity has apparently become contaminated with European paganism and has, over the centuries, become something different and incomparable with the first century Christianity. This is not an attack on the older denominations nor is it a criticism of their beliefs and practices. In fact, they have done the spade work and have invested heavily in mission and evangelism particularly taking the Christian mission from Europe to other parts of the world. But human efforts cannot adequately fulfil the plans of God and the demands of His kingdom.

The Quest for thaumaturgy

What is missing in today's Christianity and how can the church regain its old glory? It looks like the church has lost its faith and really needs to reposition itself by working hard to recover the crescendo of faith with prayers and fasting for the return of Apostolic powers bestowed on the first Apostles especially at the Pentecost phenomenon. It should be recognised that these powers for signs and wonders were bestowed not as a once and for all phenomenon as most people believe today; but as a perpetual grace still available to be activated by all ardent believers. This is the very reason why the Holy Spirit triggered revivals in different parts of the world during the 19th and 20th centuries. Signs and wonders are essential tools for successful mission and evangelism. Without these, the church of Christ would look like cooked meals on the table that omitted the crucial ingredient of salt. How can the eater find the meal tasteful and delicious and desirable without the important ingredient?

The former British Prime Minister, Margaret Thatcher once described her ministers who could not deliver expected standard of services as 'wet' and lacking the 'umph' -meaning that they lacked the 'spark' as the targets from their ministries fell short of high expectations. Such ministers needed to be upgraded by whatever means to deliver positive results if they must justify holding on to their portfolios. The same exercise is required in our churches today in order to return to active working of the Holy Spirit. Did Jesus not give the assurance that:

'these signs shall follow them that believe; in my name shall they cast out devils; they shall speak with new tongues; they shall take up serpents; and if they drink any deadly thing, it shall not hurt them; they shall lay hands on the sick, and they shall recover'(Mk.16:17/18)

Signs and wonders can return to the church or believers only if sincere belief is restored. The belief must be anchored on the solid Rock. That Rock is Jesus who described Himself as the vine and the church or believers as branches.

He that abideth in me, and I in him, the same bringeth forth much fruit; for without me ye can do nothing. If a man abide not in me, he is cast forth as a branch, and is withered; and men gathered them, and cast them into the fire, and they are burned. (St John 15: 5,6)

Can the above come alive again in the life of the church? This again is a matter of faith. It has worked out perfectly for those who believe. Jesus gave the assurance that

'if thou canst believe, all things are possible to him that believeth' (Mk 9:23).

This is why many Revivals as outlined above have demonstrated that with faith, all things are possible. Signs and wonders have littered many of their ministries. Even in ordinary life experience, faith has worked wonders in many peoples' lives.

Denominational Gifts and Specialisations

For every organisation there is always a mission statement that is implied or expressly stated. For Cherubim & Seraphim Church, it is implied in its ethos of deliverance, healing, evangelism, praise and worship. Deliverance and healing go together and will be so treated. The C & S can conveniently be perceived as belonging to the military wing of Christianity. As there are different functions in the machinery of any government such as, inter alia, The Treasury, Foreign Affairs, Home Affairs, Defence, Health, Welfare, Education, Trade and Commerce. Also, as there are different functions of the Angels in heaven such as messengers of peace, like Archangel Gabriel; and of war, like Archangel Michael; so also on earth there are different functions of the various denominations such as the Quakers for peace, the Salvation Army for relief of poverty and suffering, the Missionary Societies for evangelism; so is the Cherubim & Seraphim for deliverance and healing in addition to evangelism, praise and worship. This description of C & S epistemology is synonymous to the mission statement of our Lord as outlined by Isaiah:

'The spirit of the Lord God is upon me; because the Lord hath anointed me to preach good tidings unto the meek; he hath sent me to bind up the broken hearted, to proclaim liberty to the captives, and the opening of the prison to them that are bound; to proclaim the acceptable year of the Lord and the day of vengeance of our God; to comfort all that mourn; to appoint unto them that mourn in Zion, to give unto them beauty for ashes, the oil of joy for mourning, the garment of praise for the spirit of heaviness, that they might be called trees of righteousness, the planting of the Lord, that he might be glorified' (Is.61:1-3).

When we say we are engaged in the ministry of deliverance, it should be asked, deliverance from what? The starting point for deliverance is the awareness that there are forces visible and invisible impacting on our lives whether we believe it or not. It is true that many of our health problems in life are self-inflicted such as over- or under-eating and drinking, eating and/or drinking unhealthy substances, carelessness in eating and drinking etc. The consequences could be uncomfortable, resulting in headaches, stomach disorder or the like. But there are others that cannot be explained literally or even scientifically. Such causations are explainable only by spiritual discernment and they have to be fought against through spiritual battle. The weapons for the spiritual battle are none other than faith, prayer and fasting. That is what Paul had in mind when he declared that:

'we wrestle not against flesh and blood, but against principalities, against powers, against the rulers of the darkness of this world, against spiritual wickedness in high places' (Eph. 6:12) . . . 'above all, taking the shield of faith, wherewith ye shall be able to quench all the fiery darts of the wicked. And take the helmet of salvation, and the sword of the Spirit, which is the word of God.'(16/17).

All these forces are invisible and unless there is spiritual direction to counteract their wicked plans, the victims could perish (Prov. 29:18). Paul was one of the first to recognise that other forces that are invisible necessarily impact on our lives. The Christian believer should not always take things for granted. He must always watch and pray. Complete deliverance cannot be won without the supplementary spiritual battle. That is why reliance on medical solutions and/or traditional herbal remedies will not always result in complete deliverance. There is always something missing to complete the equation. The missing component is none other than faith, prayer and fasting. The Cherubim & Seraphim doctrine is not averse to the use of medication and/or traditional herbal remedies. These in most cases do help to provide temporary solutions. The perfect and lasting solution comes only from God who hears and answers prayers. Jesus let us know that

'whosoever drinketh of the water that I shall give him shall never thirst; but the water that I shall give him shall be in him a well of water springing up into everlasting life' (John 4:14).

Deliverance and Healing

This process in the Cherubim & Seraphim and some other Aladura churches takes the form of modern military operations. In a full scale operation in modern warfare, all the arms of defence are employed: the Army on the ground, the Navy on the sea and the Air Force in the sky. Communication between these competences results in powerful assault on the enemy to achieve victory. A similar scenario is true of war on the wiles of the devil to secure deliverance and healing. Prayers are said by Prayerists (Prayer Warriors or Aladuras) with the guidance of visions and revelations (delivered by Visioners) which give directives for the modality of prayer to be said. The combination of these competences will always result in a formidable assault on forces of adversity and yield an awesome result in victory and success.

The modality could take the form of giving answers to the six questions: what, why, when, where, how, who. In other words, what scriptures to be read, why they should be read, when they should be read, where they should be read, the frequency of the reading, how they should be read, and who should do the readings. The Prayerists or Prayer Warriors are usually ordained Elders from within the five-hierarchy model of ministry: Teachers, Pastors, Evangelists, Prophets and Apostles. They should be active and energetic volunteers who are prepared to fight any spiritual battle through faith, prayer and fasting, to engage in spiritual warfare and to deliver victory in the name of Christ.

Deliverance and healing are applicable to victims who can be either physically or mentally ill. Physical illness is easier to identify as they come through pain, weakness and disability; but mental illness is more difficult to discern as the manifestation appears at different levels, from mild to severe. There are many victims of mental illness that appear normal to the naked eye; but their lifestyles always show that something is not right. The Bible says that 'by their fruits, ye shall know them' (Matt.7:20); it also speaks of

The arrow that flieth by day, . . . the pestilence that walketh in darkness . . . the destruction that wasteth at noonday' (Ps. 91: 5/6).

Victims to these evils need to come 'under the shadow of the Almighty' where they shall find refuge under His wings, and His truth shall be their 'shield and buckler'(verse 4). These verses provide the framework from where Prayer Warriors (Aladuras) can pitch their spiritual battle.

Faith

This is an essential tool in prayer if the Christian believer must fight spiritual battles and win. *'Faith is the substance of things hoped for, the evidence of things not seen' (Hebrews 11:1)*. One of the strong recommendations of Jesus himself to his disciples was to grow in faith. He often rebuked them for not having enough faith. David did not confront Goliath without the essential tool of faith. Similarly, Daniel could not survive the dreadful danger to his life in the lions' den. Shadrach, Meshack and Abednego had strong faith to survive the danger of fire of Nebuchadnezza's furnace.

'Be strong in the Lord, and in the power of his might. Put on the whole armour of God, that ye may be able to stand against the wiles of the devil' (Eph. 6:10-11).

David did not put on the armour of man. In fact, it was too heavy for him. He opted instead to put on the armour of God (which enabled him to become bold and courageous), went into the battle and won the miraculous victory that earned him the enviable praise of the nation of Israel. The Christian believer today requires the faith of David to 'be able to stand against the wiles of the devil' Paul perceived faith as a shield,

'wherewith ye shall be able to quench all the fiery darts of the wicked' Eph. 6:16).

Jesus gave the assurance that even a little measure of faith can work wonders.

'If ye have faith as a grain of mustard seed; ye shall say unto this mountain, remove hence to yonder place; and it shall remove; and

nothing shall be impossible unto you. Howbeit, this kind goeth not out but by prayer and fasting' (Matt. 17:20-21).

In today's Western societal lifestyle, the necessity for faith has been heavily eroded by the affluence of life and the advancement of science and technology, and the sophistication of medical solutions. In Africa on the other hand, the latter is available on a limited scale and hence, reliance on faith healing has dominated the thinking of that society. In most cases, medical options only come as the solution of last resort. The African diaspora in the West therefore, finds it odd that the society is almost entirely bereaved of faith in the day to day spiritual living where they live outside Africa. However, whether or not the African is spiritually advantaged remains to be seen as time goes on, and as the continent catches up with the West in science and technology. If their faith is built on the rock (Jesus is the rock), it shall never fail, science or no science; technology or no technology; affluence or no affluence.

Prayer and fasting

Faith alone cannot win a spiritual battle. Prayer and fasting are necessary components to boost the element of faith. Paul recommends 'Praying always with all prayer and supplication in the Spirit' (Eph. 6:18). He perceives prayer as 'the helmet of salvation, and the sword of the Spirit, which is the word of God' (6:17). Prayer and fasting cannot be divorced from faith in the process of deliverance and healing. It is the combination coupled with the mercy of God that gives rise to the efficacy of prayer, which is the hallmark of the Aladura. In the Cherubim & Seraphim and other Aladura churches, members are given time during worship to give open testimonies and to publish how the power of prayer has worked wonders in their lives. Many have testified of numerous miraculous occurrences in the congregational worship which often trigger shouts of hallelujahs, singing praises and rejoicings in the knowledge that signs and wonders that dominated the New Testament narratives are neither extinct nor have they become historical in context, but can still be reactivated into practicality.

I once challenged a gathering of ecumenical delegates from many parts of the world in Geneva in the early 80s to wake up to the power of the Holy Spirit. An Orthodox priest from Eastern Europe reminded me that what I was preaching was not a new discovery of the Africans, but that the Holy Spirit is the property of the Church universal. All that was needed was to reactivate the energy and restore the ethereal powers of the Holy Spirit of God. I agreed with him.

Models of Prayer

There are different forms of prayer models and the Cherubim & Seraphim embrace them all. Beginning from Judaism, different models have emerged into Christianity and I would like to outline a comprehensive one by Bob Young (Ministry & Mission) outlining Five Models: **ACTS, PARTS, Five-Finger, TRIP & Divine**[58]

ACTS

- A—Adoration : praising God for who He is
- C—Confession: owning our sins
- T—Thanksgiving: thanking God for all He has done
- S—Supplication: prayers of request for ourselves and others.

---

58 *www.bobyoungresources.com/articles/prayer-models.htm*

PARTS

- P—Praise
- A—Ask
- R—Repent
- T—Thank
- S—Share

FIVE-FINGER

- Thumb: pray for those closest to you
- Pointing finger: pray for those who guide us: teachers, doctors, counsellors, mentors
- Middle finger (tallest one): pray for those who lead us: government, civic, business leaders, police and firefighters.
- Ring finger (weakest one): pray for those who are weak, poor, sick, disabled, infants, homeless, the powerless, the persecuted
- Pinkie (the smallest, the least): pray for myself

TRIP

- T—For what am I Thankful?
- R—What do I Regret?
- I—Intercession—for whom do I need to pray?
- P—What is my Purpose or Plan?

DIVINE READING

One method of building an effective prayer life includes Bible reading and prayer as complementary parts of one's devotional life. Sometimes referred to as 'divine reading', it may be compared to feasting on the word of God. The four steps are reading the Bible (taking a bite), meditating on it (chewing), praying (savouring the word), and contemplating its applications so it becomes a part of ones's life (digesting).

- Reading. Read the passage slowly. Pay attention to the text. Read it several times. Underline sections that catch your attention.

- Meditating. Try to grasp the meaning of the passage, be aware of God's presence in your life.

- Praying. Respond to God, converse with him about the passage and his will. Open your heart to God. Share your heart, not a laundry list of needs or things you think you ought to pray about.

- Contemplating. Focus on God, rest in his presence, and commit yourself to living out his will, especially as reflected in the reading.

This method allows the Christian to interact with God and with the Word of God, to know the Bible, self, others and God through the eyes of a developing faith.

It looks like Bob Young had in depth knowledge of Cherubim & Seraphim epistemology in his analysis. Virtually all of his outline feature in our liturgy especially on Divine Worship on Sundays. The generality of our worship from the Opening Prayers through

Thanksgiving Prayers, Intercession Prayers (Three Peoples' Prayers), Congregational Prayers and Closing Prayers, all the above analysis have always found a place in our prayer offerings.

Silent Prayers

Prayers could be silent and members are encouraged to employ this mode especially at the close of Service before the Benediction is pronounced. It is recognised that Hannah employed this mode although Eli the priest could not understand why; but God did understand and answered her prayer (I Sam, 1:13). Silent prayers can also be used by individuals when on their own or in company of other people but with the desire to make the prayer private and personal. This prevents delay in praying at the appropriate time. Such prayers can be silent, quick and straight to the point without beating about the bush.

Individual Prayers

Secondly, prayers could be individualised. Sometimes, an individual Elder could be appointed to pray for a particular purpose either in the congregation of worshippers or anywhere else. Some Elders are spiritually gifted to pray for efficacy and such Elders are often encouraged to pray for different purposes. Subsequent open testimonies by recipients of such prayers is the proof that such Elders are specially gifted and anointed.

Congregational Prayers

Third, prayers could be said by engaging the whole congregation who pray simultaneously. Such congregational prayers are often said very loudly and powerfully, akin to the prayer of the Hebrews at the fall of the walls of Jericho (Jos. 6:16). Sometimes, seven Elders are appointed to say a prayer. The number seven has powerful spiritual significance and more will be said about numbers in another chapter. The invasion of Jericho, for instance, took seven days and prayers were said everyday until the seventh day when the prayers were said seven times; and on the seventh time, the prayers were directed to be said very loudly and the miracle happened as the walls of the city fell.

The methodology could differ from time to time as the Spirit directs. Sometimes, if the prayer is for a single person or a group of people, seven Elders could be asked to form a circle, sometimes holding hands and with the people receiving the prayer in the middle, prayers are said loudly and sealed[59] by an Elder. Sometimes, prayers could be said on consecrated water for drinking or for washing or for sprinkling.

Sprinkling and anointing

Sometimes again, a prayer could involve the sprinkling and anointing with oil.[60] Occasionally, the whole congregation is sprinkled with consecrated water and anointed with olive oil in a protection service. It is believed that the mark of God is on them whenever this sacramental is ministered just as the Israelites received anointing with blood in Egypt for protection. In a wave of destruction on the land, the angels of the Lord passed over those who received the anointment. Anointing with oil also has the effect of forgiveness of

---

59 The habit of sealing prayers will be explained in a later chapter on the uniqueness of C & S.

60 Again, the ritual of sprinkling and anointing will be explained in a later chapter.

sins and healing. That is why James the Apostle urged those who are afflicted to

'call for the elders of the church; and let them pray over him, anointing him with oil in the name of the Lord; and the prayer of faith shall save the sick, and the Lord shall raise him up; and if he has committed sins, they shall be forgiven him' (James 5:14-15).

The Essence of Prayer

Prayer is the direct and shortest way to communicate with God. The greater the frequency of prayers, the nearer to God for answered prayers will be. The deeper the degree of faith in prayers, the more effective the prayers will be. James tells us that

'the effectual fervent prayers of a righteous man availeth much' (James 5:16).

It is an understatement to point out that Jesus certainly laid the example to pray very often, sometimes with his disciples and sometimes on his own in liaising with his Father. Even though he did not really need to do so as the Son of God, but principally to show his disciples of the necessity to prioritise prayer in their daily activities.

Those who pray often for whatever reason should always remember that God will not answer the prayers of sinners without absolution. God is holy and will not interact with sin. Therefore, forgiveness of sins must essentially precede communication with God. This is the importance of intercession of Jesus and the cross, from where sinners' faults are washed before their prayers can be heard and answered. From the point of washing, the sinner becomes blessed. God will listen to those who are blessed. Those who are blessed have escaped the wrath of God by Law; and have come under cover of absolution by Grace.

'Blessed is he whose transgression is forgiven, whose sin is covered (Ps. 32:1).

This is the advantage of the benevolence of God. He

'will have mercy unto whom He will have mercy, and I will have compassion on whom I will have compassion' (Rom 8:15).

Evangelism

This is central to the theology of Cherubim & Seraphim in a different way. In the Nigerian context, Evangelism is not only done on the pulpit but also regularly outdoors in the early mornings by prophets and prophetesses holding their Bibles and Hand Bells. The Evangelists travel a predetermined number of streets by foot in the early mornings ringing their bells as they go and preaching to residents who could hear gospel messages at home before they go out to earn their daily bread. Even travellers in the buses and cars hear the word of God as they travel to work. This mode of evangelism is possible only in Africa where there is no law forbidding them to do so. Such a mode of evangelising would be perceived as disturbing public peace in Western countries.

Outdoor evangelism can also take the form of singing and preaching in convenient locations like public parks and the seaside where the public go for relaxation or sometimes to witness any events of interest. Those who care to listen to the word of God gather round for the opportunity and those who are not interested please themselves with other engagements. Through this method of evangelism, many people give themselves to Christ and are enlisted for baptism. Most Aladura churches engage in this kind of evangelism as a means of recruiting adherents to their membership. Evangelism is done randomly throughout the year but essentially regularly at Easter when early in the morning inspired Evangelists parade the streets ringing handbells and proclaiming 'Christ the Lord is risen today!'. This message is repeated severally along the street for everyone to hear in their homes; passers-by and travellers also benefit from the proclamations. The message is received with joy among the Christian communities throughout the country prior to the Easter worship in the different churches.

Praise and Worship

As the Cherubim & Seraphim church delights in signs and wonders as a means of promoting the growth of the church, there is always congregational rejoicing when beneficiaries come out to testify of the result of prayers and how God's mercy has brought to their lives deliverance and healing, reconciliation, protection, direction of the Holy Spirit, provision for their needs, promotion at work, success and victory in their undertakings to mention a few. For all these and other reasons, songs of praise abound with melodious music and dancing to the glory of God for His mercies.

Individuals who come out for open testimonies sometimes come with their own choice songs of praise to the Lord and the congregation join with them. Sometimes, they simply tell their success stories and the Choir leads in singing an appropriate song of praise. At other occasions, the Choir simply leads a session of praise and worship by introducing numerous songs and choruses either on their own or with the entire congregation. Praise and worship is one aspect of the Cherubim & Seraphim theology that gives members the joy of refreshing their spirits at worship after the stress of daily work and unpleasant encounters in their daily lives. Praise and worship is characterised by good music, clapping and dancing. The choir is usually equipped with different drums, organs, pianos, keyboards, guitars, trumpets, tambourines, and depending on the culture of the worshippers, anything that facilitates good music as psalm 150 puts it,

'praise him with the sound of the trumpet; praise him with the psaltery and harp. Praise him with the timbrel and dance; praise him with stringed instruments and organs, praise him upon the loud cymbals;praise him upon the high sounding cymbals; let everything that hath breath praise the Lord . . . '

Praise and worship is one of the strong elements of inculturation in the theology of the Cherubim & Seraphim. Many aspects of worship which includes African music which in the missionary days would be considered non-Christian are now common features in our praise and worship. One verse of a C & S song goes:

> *Which Christian faith shall end the world?*
> *Cherubim and Seraphim Band.*
> *In like manner as Noah's Ark;*
> *Cherubim and Seraphim Band*[61]

---

[61] 'Cherubim and Seraphim Band' here means Cherubim and Seraphim Church. The word 'Church' only became used after maturity of the 'Band' or 'Society' by graduation into 'Church' status at the point of registration. Initially, the church was started as a form of club of inter-denominational believers in the efficacy of prayer. Most of the early songs of C & S, therefore, used the word 'Band' or 'Society' rather than 'Church'.

Cherubim & Seraphim Epistemology

At the beginning before I was converted to the faith, I wondered how the prophecy of this song was going to happen! I interpreted the song to mean that the Cherubim & Seraphim would have to take over the other Christian denominations for this to happen. It looked to me as an impossibility for such a new and insufficiently equipped player in ecumenism to emerge as a predator with the potential to acquire the bigger, stronger and older players in the ecumenical community and to play a leading role in ecclesiological worship. But I was wrong in my assessment! Now I can see that it will never happen that way. But rather surprisingly, and for the past few decades, by stealth, the take-over is taking place in most Christian denominations! It is not that the latter have been acquired under the control of C&S administratively, but that they are gradually adopting the epistemology of C&S. In most churches in Nigeria and elsewhere globally today, the acquisition is becoming evident in the shouting of Hallelujah; there is clapping of hands during songs; there are native drummings, even the 'talking drums' hung on the shoulder; there is moving around in dancing to the praise of God.

Now it is becoming more and more difficult to differentiate between the worship of C&S and other Christian denominations, including the older missionary church denominations in worship. It is now that the words of the song, 'Which Christian faith shall end the world' mean something to the hearers. The Cherubim & Seraphim may not yet be perceived as taking over other denominations, but it is certain its epistemology is increasingly gaining upper hand ecclesiologically.

Places of prayer

Prayers can be said anywhere and anytime, silently or audibly as it may be convenient. St Paul recommends 'praying always with all prayer and supplication in the Spirit' (Eph. 6:18). One Cherubim & Seraphim song goes:

'Pray, always pray, the Holy Spirit pleads, within thee all my daily hourly needs...'

That is the reason why prayer should not be limited to when believers go to church or at other formalised times, morning and evening at home. Prayer should be said as needed as above anytime and anywhere, *'within thee all my daily hourly needs'* But in addition, prayers can be said in the fashion of the habit of Jesus who went alone or in company of selected aides to special sites:

On the mountain

Whenever private prayer is needed, Jesus always went to the top of the mountain to pray. In Cherubim & Seraphim particularly in Nigeria, several mountains are so used. Apart from individual visits to the mountains for prayers, there are also regular visits by members. An example is the Cherubim & Seraphim Movement Church congregating on 'Mount Horeb' in Kaduna for weeklong prayers during May annually. The annual visit is open to members who can afford the time and the journey from all over the world. Most prophets and prophetesses of the church usually find their way to the mountain for retreat, prayers and worship.

Because of the spiritual significance of the mountain many congregations name their Prayer Houses after a mountain: Mount

Horeb, Mount Zion, Mount Sinai and others. Even when mountain names run out, and in order not to duplicate the names of other congregations, they resort to such names as Mount of Peace, Mount of Salvation, Mount of Joy, Mount of Miracles, Mount of Victory and the like. Praying from the mountain top will always be popular as it is one of the places where the world can be seen as insignificant, and heavenly values and awareness are highlighted.

By the Seaside

Very often and at any time, the Cherubim & Seraphim along with some of the other Aladura churches find their way to the seaside to worship and to offer prayers for general or specific purposes. Such visits to the seaside are sometimes directed by visions and sometimes regularly as a habit by some members. Some spend short hours and some, long, depending on individual needs. The sea is perceived as one of the wonderful works of God. When one faces the sea and and looks in awe how extensive the water can be as if there is no end to it, the work of God becomes apparent and one's spirituality heightens beyond imagination. Facing the sea means turning ones' back to the world. The world becomes very little and insignificant and the power of God becomes magnified.

The same effect is true when one travels by air. On looking down from the windows of an aircraft when passing over a city, some mighty buildings as seen from the sky become so small and insignificant. As the aircraft flies above the clouds, it would look as if the world is turned upside down; whereas one looks up to view the clouds from the ground, but on the aircraft flying above the clouds, one has to look down. All these show the wonderful works of God and His power and might become awesome and magnified. In these times of appreciation of the work of God, the prayer of the believer is facilitated with the convictions of the magnitude of the wisdom and creative power of the Almighty God.

In the Wilderness

Depending on proximity to members, the wilderness is an alternative to the seaside and the mountain. In Nigeria, one site or the other is always accessible and members take advantage of whatever site is convenient to them. In each of the above secluded places, the advantage is that one is physically separated from the vanity of the world and left alone or in company of other believers to concentrate on spirituality. By so doing, many have received the anointing of the Holy Spirit in various formats. Some begin to speak in tongues; some receive the gift of interpretation; some begin to see visions; some, the gift of prophecy; some the gift of praying with fire and authority for efficacy; some receive the gift of discernment.

The list is not exhaustive and it is incredible what visiting members can receive in these special environments. This habit of going to secluded places for prayer is similar to what the monks do especially in the Egyptian Coptic and Ethiopian Orthodox Churches. It is biblical and especially exemplified in the life of our Lord, Jesus Christ. Keen observers will be able to see many things in the wilderness to appreciate the awesomeness of the works of God. There will be seen, birds singing on the tree, small animals on the ground, even ants that group themselves and parade like an army of soldiers, with some kind of Generals or Inspectors marching alongside the troops! Many things to convince the doubters that God is mighty and that His works are wonderful can be found in the wilderness.

Understanding of pneumatology in C & S Epistemology

Pneumatology is a discipline in Christian theology that focuses on the study of the Holy Spirit. The term derives from the Greek word 'pneuma' which designates 'breath' or 'spirit' and metaphorically describes a non-material being or influence.

The knowledge of the Holy Spirit and the deployment of His power especially in prayers is of paramount importance in Cherubim & Seraphim epistemology. Jesus warned believers:

'for without me ye can do nothing' (John 15:5).

This statement is a confirmation of Zechariah's prophecy

'Not by might, nor by power, but by my spirit, saith the Lord of hosts' (Zech. 4:6).

Most members of C & S desire to receive the Holy Spirit, especially at baptism. Water baptism (by immersion) in the church is limited to members from the age of twelve. That means in effect that the church adopts 'Believers' Baptism' whilst infants are accorded 'Christening' or 'Blessing' from the age of eight days at home or in the Prayer House as mutually convenient to the parents and clergy.

Concerning water baptism by immersion, most members aspire to receive the Holy Spirit before, during or immediately after the immersion as it happened to Jesus at his own occasion at the River Jordan. Many candidates even ask for it in prayer and fasting. Quite a few such prayers are answered but most have to wait if they were destined to be so baptised. Classical Pentecostalism asserts that speaking in tongues is the initial evidence of baptism by the Holy Spirit. Many are even baptised and never experience receiving the Spirit in the form of speaking in tongues. This cannot be a surprise as the Bible says

'many are called, but a few are chosen.(Matt.22:14; 20:16).

This disparity leads to two schools of thought in Christian theology. The teaching of the Synoptic Gospels, especially Luke (who also authored the Book of Acts) on the one hand; and of Paul, (who wrote most of the Epistles in the New Testament) on the other. For the purpose of clarification, it would be helpful to identify where both authors agree. Both are in agreement that the reception of the Holy Spirit by a convert happens only once. What is included in the reception is where they differ. The point of contention is what constitutes conversion-initiation, and how the latter relates to faith, repentance, water baptism and reception of the Holy Spirit.[62]

Prophetic Pneumatology

Luke apparently takes to the two stage process of John the Baptist (Mk.1:8). This model effectively separates water baptism from Spirit baptism. Further evidence can be cited from the Samaritan 'mini Pentecost' (Acts 8:16) and the Ephesian twelves' water and Spirit baptism (Acts 19). Exegetes have therefore described Luke's thoughts on Spirit reception as Prophetic pneumatology. This means water baptism in the first instance, followed by Spirit baptism at a later time. The second stage completes the conversion-initiation process of the Christian convert. Proponents of this

---

[62] Adegoke, John O ,Pneumatology of Mission, *MA Assignment Module 402.1 2005 p8*

view such as the denominations where Water Baptism is followed by Confirmation and/or the laying on of hands support the idea of the conversion being 'regenerated' at the point of faith, repentance and water baptism. At the laying on of hands, the convert receives the Holy Spirit for empowerment for service and mission.

John the Baptist clearly distinguished the two forms of baptism. He acknowledged that his own function was to baptise converts by water. His baptism did not include the higher and final model which is Spirit baptism, and which according to him must wait for Jesus, who he humbly regarded as his higher authority. This perception of pneumatology is evident in the process of baptism in Catholic and Orthodox denominations where the Priests conduct water baptisms and the Bishops, the Confirmation rituals. In these denominations the converts qualify for participation in the Holy Communion after the laying on of hands by the Bishop in Confirmation.

Sotereological Pneumatology

As opposed to the Lukan concept, Paul insists that conversion-initiation is or should be a single process for the convert. This means that the four elements of faith, repentance, water baptism and the gift of the Holy Spirit should not be capable of separation in a Christian convert. According to a renowned theologian and writer, James Dunn,

'no christian was unbaptised, but not all those baptised were ipso facto Christians. No Christian was without the Spirit, for only those who had (received) the Spirit were ipso facto Christians.[63]

---

63 James D G Dunn, *Baptism in the Holy Spirit*, London SCM 1973, P228

Paul's assertion derives from his letter to the Romans (8:9b)

'Now if any man have not the Spirit of Christ, he is none of his'

Paul's concept of Spirit reception is, therefore, described as 'Sotereological Pneumatology'[64] According to this assertion, both water and spirit baptism should essentially come together in one package. Perhaps the argument could be backed by the baptism of Jesus in the River Jordan, immediately after which a voice came from heaven to validate the ritual and the Holy Spirit descended on him in the form of a dove (Matt.3:16-17).

In view of all the arguments, it is necessary to explain that many denominations tend to adopt one position or the other. In an inter-denominational Seminar, I was tasked to explain where exactly the Cherubim & Seraphim stood. My answer was complex. In my experience, I have witnessed several where both Lukan and Pauline concepts came true. It is not because their differences have been resolved. It is simply because in baptism, what can be simple for one person can prove difficult for another. In some cases, candidates have been baptised in C&S and whilst some receive both water and spirit, some others are not so privileged. In practical terms, our baptism should be described as soteriological because baptised members qualify for and receive the Holy Communion immediately after their baptism whether or not they have been endowed with Spirit baptism.

God always works in mysterious ways. The experience of the baptism of Cornelius, where reception of the Spirit came before water baptism shows that 'God is no respecter of persons' (Acts 10:34). Certainly, God is no respecter of traditions either. As the

---

64 Turner Max, *Journal of Pentecostal Theology*, 15(1999), p16

expectation of the Apostles was that water baptism should precede spirit baptism and they were proved wrong, so is the distinction between Prophetic and Soteriological perspectives spiritually baseless and unnecessary. In this discourse, it is an understatement to say that God does not follow human formular and He is ipso facto neither 'prophetic' nor 'soteriological' because His works are always incomprehensible.

The Cherubim & Seraphim perception of the sotereological pneumatology is that it is not impossible for anyone to be blessed with both baptisms on the same occasion. God's blessings come in different forms and shapes. Either water and/or Spirit baptisms can lead believers to salvation. Falling in spirit and speaking in tongues does not necessarily lead to salvation. Evidence of thaumaturgy and ethereal gifts does not necessarily lead to salvation. In the end, it is only through the grace of God and through His benevolent disposition that salvation can be granted.

In the Sermon on the mountain, Jesus did make clear:

Not everyone that saith unto me, Lord, Lord, shall enter into the kingdom of heaven; but he that doeth the will of my Father which is in heaven. Many will say to me in that day, Lord, Lord, have we not prophesied in thy name? and in thy name have cast out devils? and in thy name done many wonderful works? And then will I profess unto them, I never knew you: depart from me ye that work iniquity. (Matt.7:21-23)

So, speaking in tongues, prophesying, preaching and all other gifts of the Holy Spirit do not necessarily lead anyone to the kingdom of heaven. Therefore, the assertion of Paul that 'if any man has not the Spirit of Christ, he is none of his' cannot mean that the man should possess all the gifts to qualify for entry into the kingdom of God. It is rather what Jesus hinted that the entry will be limited to 'he that doeth the will of my Father which is in heaven'. This is the understanding and the position in Cherubim & Seraphim Epistemology.

Sotereological pneumatology as claimed by Paul, therefore, could not have meant that the initial evidence of speaking in tongues must be visible and recognisable by all as a criteria for salvation and entry to the kingdom of heaven. If that is what Paul meant, he would then be contradicting himself as he taught of the diversity of gifts and asking:

Are all apostles? Are all Prophets? Are all teachers? Are all workers of miracles? Have all the gifts of healing? Do all speak with tongues? Do all interpret? (I Cor. 12:29-30)

Angelology in C & S Theology

There has been widespread misunderstanding of angels in the C&S epistemology and the topic requires careful explanation. It cannot be denied that the names Cherubim & Seraphim are angelic names. That does not imply automatically that the C&S worship angels as some critics do allege. It should be understood that angels themselves refuse to be worshipped because they too worship God as we do. When John the disciple (who wrote the Book of Revelations) fell at the feet of an angel to worship him, the angel rebuked him and said:

See thou do it not: I am thy fellow servant, and of thy brethren that have the testimony of Jesus: worship God: for the testimony of Jesus is the spirit of prophecy (Rev.19:10)

Cherubim & Seraphim Epistemology

The angel was quite right as worship of any angel will amount to breaking the second commandment of God (Ex.20:4-5). Even though angels are created higher beings than humans; and endowed with more ethereal powers, they remain obedient to the worship of God, unlike Lucifer that got out of control and rebelled against God. God has made man 'a little lower than the angels' according to Psalm 8:5. Therefore, there is very little difference between angels and humans and in fact, a righteous man will be enabled to judge even the angels in the kingdom of heaven. The testimony of the angel is reaffirmed a second time saying:

See thou do it not: for I am thy fellow servant, and of thy brethren the prophets, and of them which keep the sayings of this book: worship God. (Rev.22:9)

The angel in the quotations made it clear that it is God only that deserves to be worshipped and glorified, nobody else. This is the theology of Cherubim & Seraphim and nobody can claim that angels are worshipped in the church or anywhere else. Having said that, some critics point out that in some C&S churches, the altar areas are decorated with inscriptions on the walls reading Holy Holy Holy Lord God Almighty with the Cross in between two angels; and that the worship leader faces these images to worship them. The simple answer to that is that the inscriptions are quotations directly from Revelation 4:8, describing how the heavenly hosts (including Cherubim & Seraphim) worship around the throne of God. It is the Lord's Prayer that prompts C&S members to activate:

'Thy will be done in earth, as it is in heaven'. (Matt.6:10).

Moreover, the idea of the worship leader facing the altar is simply to enable him to focus and avoid distraction during the divine

Service; neither the worship leader nor anybody else worship images as alleged by certain critics. In fact, this practice of the worship leader facing the altar is not a hard and fast rule, and some C&S churches do not even observe it at all.

Unlike some denominations, the Cherubim & Seraphim Churches do not encourage mounting images of Saints on the walls of our Prayer Houses, not even the image of Jesus nor of Mary, the mother of Jesus. On the other hand, the Bible tells us that the redeemed believers who shall reign with Christ will be empowered to judge not only the unrighteous, but they will also be empowered to 'judge angels' in His kingdom (ICor 6:3). This power over angels of course refers to fallen angels because man was created 'a little lower than the angels' whether fallen or not. This is why man is empowered to fight 'not only against flesh and blood (human beings) but against principalities, against powers, against the rulers of the darkness of this world, against spiritual wickedness in high places'.

Who exactly are angels?

Angels are messengers of God. The Hebrew word for angel is 'malakhim' meaning, messengers. They act like postmen, delivering messages to men and executing the plans of God on divine command. Hebrews 1:14 describes them as 'ministering spirits' They are the immediate servants of God. They are the proclaimers of God's plan in the lives of men on earth. Their primary duty is to minister first to God and secondly to the anointed ones of God and to seek their interest. Daniel testified that God kindly sent an angel to the den of lions to:

'*shut the lions' mouths, that they have not hurt me*' (Daniel 6:22). The same duty is echoed in Psalm 34:7 '*The angel of the Lord encampeth round about them that fear him, and delivereth them*'. The affirmation for the same duty is also shown in Psalm 91:10-12 : '*There shall no evil befall thee, neither shall any plague come nigh thy dwelling. For he (God) shall give his angels charge over thee, to keep thee in all thy ways. They shall bear thee up in their hands, lest thou dash thy foot against a stone.*'

Most angels appear in the form of men. It is only the Cherubim and Seraphim, who are in the highest rank and surround the throne of God that are 'winged angels'. They each have six wings:

with twain they cover their faces, with twain they cover their feet and with twain they do fly (Isaiah 6:2).

The other angels have no wings. They appear to men as human beings. Such unwinged angels have appeared variously to Abraham, Isaac, Jacob, Moses and Joshua.

The 'ministering angels'

- Ministered to Hagar and Ishmael in the wilderness (Gen. 21:18)
- Baked bread for Elijah (I Kings 19:3-6)
- Ministered to Jesus after His temptation in the wilderness (Mk. 1:13)

God did not deprive the fallen angels, including Lucifer their chief, of their ethereal powers in their fall. That is why they are capable of doing both good and bad to humans in their manipulations on earth. They perform good acts to deceive, knowing that their victims would eventually be counted among their numbers when Christ shall come the second time. They are essentially anti-Christ and they already know their destiny when Jesus, the righteous Judge, shall come again to judge both the quick and the dead. Those, therefore, who invoke fallen angels to find quick solutions to their problems stand the risk of condemnation at judgement day.

CHAPTER 6

FOUNDERS OF CHERUBIM & SERAPHIM CHURCH

This Chapter, which should have been at the beginning of this book, has been deliberately shifted to the middle because of the greater emphasis given to the epistemology, rather than the founding of the church. Unlike most churches, the Cherubim & Seraphim Church was born miraculously not by design, but by the process of evolution as directed by the Holy Spirit. Two personalities were involved, despite the controversy to the contrary by some historians of the church. One argument is that Moses Orimolade Tunolase was the sole Founder. The other is that Moses Orimolade and Abiodun Akinsowon (later known as Captain Abiodun Emmanuel) spearheaded the founding of the church together. The arguments will be further analysed later after sketching the profiles of both personalities. The conclusion could well be that none of the two founded anything; and that:

'Jah Jehovah established this Great Band (Church); not by any human being'

as one of C&S choruses indicates. To further authenticate the celestial plan for the establishment of the church, one of the Cherubim & Seraphim Hymns (inspired through vision as many others) explained that it took forty years' pleading by the SON for the establishment of the Seraphim Society; and forty years for the granting of the request by the FATHER before the glorious Society was finally started. In Yoruba:

Founders of Cherubim & Seraphim Church

Ogoji odun ni BABA fi gb'ebe, ka le gb'egbe to logo yi dide;
Ogoji odun ni OMO fi bebe, lati d'egbe Serafu yi sile.

A strange prophet was born in a rural part of the country of Nigeria, at Ikare in Ondo State. One would have expected a future prophet to be born, nurtured and mentored in a Vicarage, priestly home or even in a bishopric palace. To the contrary, Moses Orimolade was born into a pagan home, whose father, named Tunolase, a renowned Traditional Healer and an Oracle Consultant in the locality; and mother, Abigail Odijoroto were idol worshippers in their prime of life. Their third child named Moses Orimolade turned out to become a prophet of God, called to Christian ministry from his mother's womb. From Orimolade's profile, the following pattern developed:

- mysterious conception, birth and childhood
- mysterious knowledge of the Scriptures despite sickly and unschooled childhood
- mysterious skills in preaching and healing
- ethereal gifts to confront and to conquer idolatry
- mysterious skills in evangelism, conversion into Christianity, baptism of converts
- referrals of converts to nearby Christian church denominations and/or
- helping to establish a church where there was none in places of ministry.

Despite the above profile, it did not occur to Orimolade that he would be at the centre of founding a church from his childhood to adulthood. In his adolescent period, he thought he was old enough to shed dependency on his parents and to find a trade to live on. Consequently, he tried his luck in different trades like farming, hunting and trading. Whilst he tried his best to develop skills in those trades in order to earn his living, in each attempt, he was always thwarted through sickness. He only found comfort and serenity when preaching and engaged in deliverance and healing ventures. His material needs were mysteriously provided without ever being engaged in any gainful employment.

This pattern of life led him through a period of about seven years into an enthusiastic crusade up and down Nigeria beginning from Ikare, his home town, and through Irun, Akongba , Oka-Akoko, Edo, Ikiran and Ibillo, Benin, and northwards through Eda, Okene, (where he helped to establish a local Anglican church), Lokoja, Ogbagi, Ayere, Ogidi, Egbe, Kabba, Abaji, Igan, Ikase, Zaria, Bauchi, Adamawa, Nguru (where he built another church), Bida. Then he continued southward through Ilorin, Ikirun (where many sick people were healed), Oshogbo, Ede, Ogbomosho, Ibadan, Abeokuta (on the invitation of the Alake), Ifako (where he was hosted by Chief Jacob Kehinde Coker), and finally arriving in Lagos Island (as guest of the Sexton, Emmanuel Olumodeji, of Holy Trinity Anglican Church, Ebute Ero on December 20, 1924) from where he proceeded to Ago Ishafia as guest of Momoh Giwa, a Muslim Leader on May 7, 1925.

Founders of Cherubim & Seraphim Church

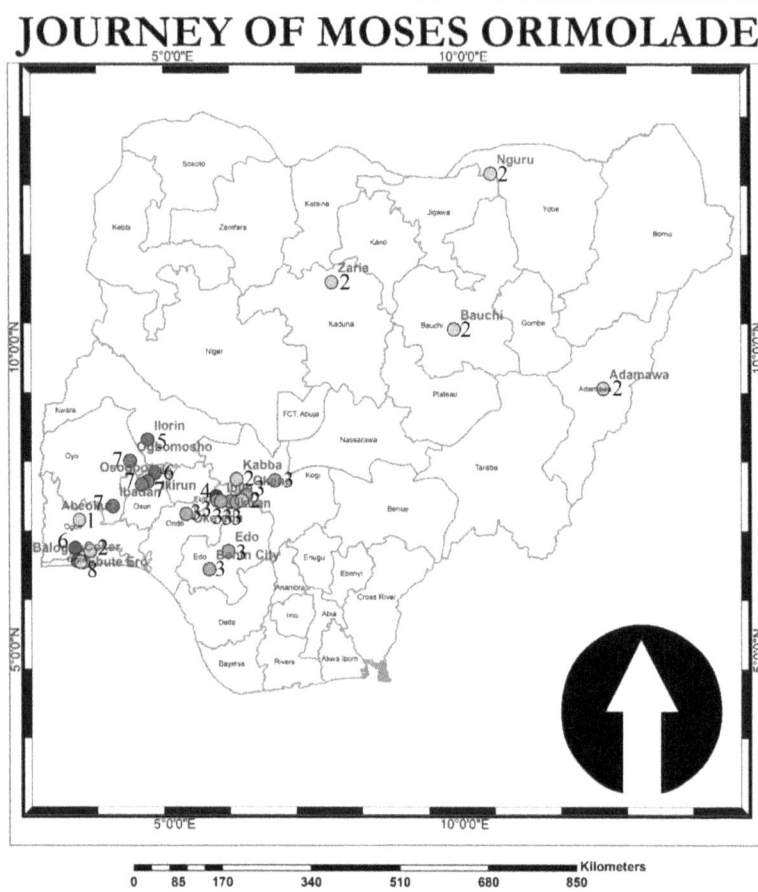

This missionary journey that took more than seven years and moving from place to place was never planned by him but simply happened mysteriously as usual. One contributing factor to this itinerary ministry was the fact that Orimolade found pleasure and comfort in articulating his gifts of preaching, evangelism, deliverance and healing ministry inside church environments, working with resident church ministers. But the latter, wherever he went, found him and his gifts distractive to their ministries; as in each case, the church members' focus and attention shifted from them to Orimolade.

This kind of paradigm shift primarily led to reluctant rejection and near expulsion of Orimolade and his ministry from church to church, and from town to town. As a result, an unplanned missionary journey emerged! Like John the Baptist and Jesus, Orimolade found company in few people who were mystified and interested in his gifts and ministry. They followed him and glorified him with the title of 'Baba Aladura', the title which many Section Heads in Cherubim & Seraphim adopt till to date.

Conception, birth and childhood

One of the mysteries during his pregnancy was how he spoke to his mother when the latter was clueless on how to lift a bundle of firewood unto her head. Suddenly, she heard a voice saying 'Don't worry, I can help you'. The mother was afraid because nobody was nearby as she looked round. She exclaimed 'who are you and where are you? The reply came back saying 'I am the baby in your womb'. Thereafter, on the next attempt, the bundle of sticks was lifted onto her head with minimal effort. Abigail then knew that she was bound to have a mysterious child on delivery.

On her delivery day, Abigail was helped by a local and experienced midwife. Immediately after delivery, the baby attempted to stand on his feet and to walk. Both mother and midwife were mystified and three times, they struggled to stop the baby as it never happened before. His father, Tunolase was alerted and he resorted to reciting incantations to stop the baby. As the midwife used force three times to prevent the baby walking, he became crippled from babyhood until his death.

Mysterious knowledge of Scriptures

Moses Orimolade did not attend any School most probably due to his disability and sickly childhood. Even though he could neither read nor write, he was extremely intelligent and knowledgeable in the Scriptures. He had passion for attending Sunday Schools and actively articulating his knowledge with learned Clergy and Sunday School Teachers. It was claimed that the Bible was mysteriously planted in his head and he was able to quote Bible passages without reading. This ability contributed to his being persistently snubbed by Clergy after Clergy; from place to place. But despite all the snubbing and unwelcome attitudes from church clergy, he was never disappointed and never gave up on preaching, deliverance and healing. The implication of persistent snubbing by a host of Clergies consequently led to his unplanned itinerary ministry up and down the country of Nigeria. This analysis suggests that Orimolade was driven to total submission to the direction of the Holy Spirit. He grew to become a determined preacher of the Word, despite undesirable obstacles.

Mysterious skills in preaching, deliverance and healing

Orimolade could preach for hours without notes and always referring to relevant Scriptures during his sermons. His sermon deliveries were so powerful and convincing that many sick people sought for, and received deliverance and healing during his crusades. It would require writing a whole book to cover important aspects of the miraculous feats by him from place to place, but let a few be mentioned as examples:

Moses Orimolade was not an ordinary prophet. He was ordained as a Prayer Warrior from his mother's womb to be a powerful prophet, spiritually equipped to fight:

'against principalities, against powers, against the rulers of the darkness of this world, against spiritual wickedness in high places' (Eph. 6:12).

After confronting idol worshippers in his hometown, including his parents, a host of converts surrendered their charms for burning; and were baptised into Christianity. At Benin City, his crusade resulted in cessation of humans for sacrifice; and recognition that human beings were created in the image of God.

Masquerades were prominent in idol worshipping in the country. Orimolade confronted them in Ikare and his life was threatened. They mounted a ferocious attack on him and his followers to put an end to his condemnation of their long-held religion. In the encounter, instead of their army fighting against Orimolade and his followers, they were confused and started killing and injuring themselves. Police intervention resulted in arresting and locking up the Orimolade's team at Kabba (the provincial Headquarters) as they were held as responsible for the assault and injuries.

Founders of Cherubim & Seraphim Church

Orimolade challenged the Police decision and with powerful prayers and preaching demanded the release of his followers. It was at that crusade that he sang the now popular C & S song:

> *E fun 'pe na kikan, ipe ihin rere;*
> *K'o dun jake, jado, l'eti gbogbo eda*
> *Chorus: Odun idasile ti de, pada, elese, pada,*
> *Odun idasile ti de, pada elese, pada.*

The above song is interpreted as

> *Blow ye the trumpet, blow; the song of liberty;*
> *Sound it loud up and down; to the hearing of all.*
> *Chorus: The year of liberty has come, repent sinners, repent*
> *The year of liberty has come, repent sinners, repent.*

Soon after this crusade, Orimolade's followers were released and they returned safely to Ikare. The battle did not end there. The idol worshippers came up with a plan to entice Orimolade with a revered title in their ranks in order to win him over. But being guided by the Holy Spirit, he declined their offer and from then, they became withdrawn and kept their distance from him.

A similar feat took place in Lagos on his arrival there. A powerful masquerader in Obun-Eko warned him not to dare come near his area to preach as he did in other areas of the city. Orimolade retorted and hinted to him of the time and date of his plan to launch his crusade in that very area. The masquerader was determined to do all within his power to disgrace Orimolade if he dared to carry out the threat. On the appointed day, as Orimolade approached the venue for the crusade, the challenger, confident of his ability to inflict wickedness and harm on Orimolade, and being fully armed with charms, started reciting pagan incantations against him. Unfortunately for him, his pagan spiritual attacks turned into a boomerang against him. He collapsed instantly and died on the spot. The masses of the witnesses were astonished and convincingly recognised that the Almighty God is more powerful than any other god and any other earthly power. Consequently, many were converted and baptised. Another song to mark the event was given on that day:

'Aje nse lasan ni, Kerubu a pa won run'

Meaning in English:

'Witches' spells are fruitless. Cherubim powers will destroy them'

Along the route of his missionary journey, Orimolade attracted masses of admirers and many sick people of various illnesses were brought to him for deliverance and healing, and many such sick people returned home with excitement and joy after their healing. Instances include a boy who accidently swallowed a needle; received prayers and subsequently vomited the needle. In another case, a woman who fell into the Lagoon in Lagos was rescued. Although the woman could not swim, but it looked like the Lagoon miraculously spewed her ashore after Orimolade prayed for her rescue.

When Orimolade's crusade reached Ogbomosho, some powerful idol worshippers conspired to expel him from their city. Their antagonism was so great that Orimolade decided to leave the city, but before leaving, he cursed the city. As a result, there was no rain in the city and pregnant women failed to deliver their babies. After a period of suffering from these curses, the Ogbomosho indigenes finally traced the prophet to Lagos and with remorse and penitence, they appealed to him to reverse the curses.

He agreed and went back to Ogbomosho with them and after his prayers, rain fell again and pregnant women resumed delivering their babies safely. All these are evidence of efficacy of prayers by a man endowed with ethereal gifts from above.

MOSES ORIMOLADE TUNOLASE

Moses Orimolade Tunolase was born either 1877 or 1879. He died in 1933. That means that he lived for either 56 or 54 years on earth. Before he was born, his father received a warning through his oracle that the child would come as an important and powerful servant of God and that his parents should exercise caution so that they would not stumble through him.

The Cherubim & Seraphim was established in 1925. That means that Orimolade's official ministry as Founder of the C&S church lasted only 8 years. But it could be claimed that his ministry started even from his mother's womb! He ministered to his mother even when he was still in the womb. First, Abigail, whilst in the bush gathering dried wood for domestic cooking, accidently dashed her foot against an obstacle. She was consoled by a voice despite being alone in the bush. She looked round but saw nobody. She was baffled and hurried out of the spot. Secondly, the mother groaned on deciding how to lift the bunch of firewood onto her head after gathering the dry woods and tying them into a bunch which was more than she could lift without struggle. His mother heard the voice again saying 'Don't worry, I can help you' but she did not see the speaker and adviser.

When she looked round and saw nobody, she shouted loudly, asking who was speaking to her. The baby replied that the voice was that of the baby in her womb. Subsequently, the heavy bunch was lifted onto her head with little or no effort. From that time, the mother, Abigail Odijoroto Tunolase knew that she would give birth to a mystery child. The bush experience confirmed that her unborn child would be a powerful servant of God as earlier revealed to her husband through an oracle.

Orimolade tried his luck on doing business as a means of earning his living. He started buying and selling palm oil and kola nuts, which trade took him and a friend with similar ambition to a town known as Oshokoshoko in Northern Nigeria. There, he had a vision warning him to abandon this ambition and to concentrate on preaching and healing. He was hesitant to obey the warning and subsequently fell ill to the point that his friend and neighbours thought that he would not survive. His friend returned to Ikare to inform his family. His brother, Egunjobi was sent to bring him back to Ikare. Miraculously, before Egunjobi reached Oshokoshoko, Orimolade had returned to Ikare, by unknown means!

The life and ministry of Moses Orimolade, Founder of Cherubim & Seraphim is modern evidence of the return of ethereal gifts to the church. Notwithstanding that he was disabled and not expected to travel long distances without stress, he still managed to travel on foot to many places, up and down the vast country of Nigeria without physical or mechanical assistance. Orimolade's movements was similar to Philip's ethereal gifts of disappearing from the Ethiopian's baptism site in the desert, and appearing on another site 'at Azotus, preaching in all the cities, till he came to Caesarea' (Acts 8: 39-40). This ethereal phenomenon was common practice in the life of Jesus around His disciples. He usually appeared and disappeared and nobody knew where He lived. He was a man of no fixed address!

Orimolade had a friend named Garuba. The latter wondered how his friend, being disabled, managed to travel to distant places on foot in record times and without distress. One day, Orimolade paid him a visit and in the evening when it was getting dark, he bade Garuba goodnight to return home. Without telling him, Garuba trailed his friend on bicycle to discover how and by what means he travelled. Orimolade was on his way, Garuba followed on bicycle but later lost sight of him. On arriving at Orimolade's house, he discovered with amazement that his limping friend travelled faster than himself riding on the bicycle!

The narratives as above are only a few out of many of Orimolade's profile to show that this man of God was endowed with ethereal gifts which resulted in supernatural feats on numerous occasions. Only a few prophets like Elijah and Elisha are so gifted in the Old Testament, and the Apostle Philip in the New. Orimolade's legacy for deployment of supernatural feats is still operating in a few C & S churches where spirituality outweighs secularism and materialism. It cannot be denied that many imposters attempt to imitate the attributes of Orimolade but through Traditional and unchristian means in order to boost their egos and to deceive many. But the Bible says 'by their fruits, ye shall know them'. They shall reap their rewards.

The imposters trying to imitate Orimolade's legacy can be likened to the seven sons of Sceva, who attempted to exorcise a demon from a man in Ephesus by using the name of Jesus as an invocation (Acts 19:14-16). The rascals met their match and ended up being injured by the demon. This practice is similar to the practice, originating in the Testament of Solomon, of invoking angels to cast out demons.[65]

Moses Orimolade was born a Nazarite as his hair grew like that of the Biblical Samson. The parents attempted to cut down his hair three times unsuccessfully. The three attempts resulted in the razor blade used breaking in pieces until they finally gave up. During his preachings, the hairs on his head very often stood up out of proportion, and most people around were astonished and frightened. He was subsequently advised to wear a hat to minimise public embarrassment of his Nazarite characteristics and outlook.

Orimolade lived a celibate life (never married and never had biological children) but very often, he made references to his children as if he had many! But today, in C&S Services, especially in celebrations, a popular song is always sung in effect, in Yoruba:

'Awa omo Mose mbo, ara aiye; awa omo Mose mbo o, ero eya.
Awa omo Mose re o ! oya.'

Meaning:

We, children of Moses are arriving, let it be announced. We, children of Moses, are here, let all be aware. We children of Moses are here, let it be acknowledged.

---

[65] Arnold, Clinton (March 2012), *Journal of the Evangelical Theological Society*, 55(1) 7-26.

The implication is that all adherents of the church are nominally children of Orimolade. That being the case, his children are apparently numberless. He did not live a barren life. More stories describing the mysterious life of this man of God could continue to fill pages and pages but such an attempt would result in writing his biography which could distort the emphasis of this book on the C&S Epistemology. So far, the story of Moses Orimolade has given no indication of his intention to found and to run any church. His greatest ambition had been to preach, to evangelise, to confront idolatry, to pray for deliverance and healing; and to baptise converts for referrals to existing Christian churches irrespective of denominations. The subsequent role as a Founder of a church did not occur to him until 1925, after his encounter with an eighteen year old lady called Christiana Abiodun Akinsowon. Even at this stage, neither Orimolade nor Captain Abiodun was thinking of the concept of 'Founder' as it subsequently emerged.

CAPTAIN CHRISTIANA ABIODUN EMMANUEL

This innocent young lady went out with friends to Campos Square in Lagos, only out to satisfy her curiosity during the Roman Catholic annual public procession of 'Corpus Christi'. She joined the crowd to watch the procession and while gazing at the Chalice in the carriage, she suddenly fell into a trance, became helpless and in a loss of emotional consciousness. Her friends helped her to return home where she continued in the trance for seven days.

She could neither eat nor drink during the period. She could not communicate in the language understood by the family but continuously spoke in unknown tongues while remaining comfortless. As speaking in an unknown tongue was first of its kind in Nigeria, the family was confused and called for help from various practitioners: Medical Doctors, Native Doctors, Herbalists young and old, and anyone else who could help to discern the cause of this strange phenomenon and to find solution to the predicament. No one of these could help. There were suggestions of confusion, madness, hallucination and such strange occurrences. Possible solutions to the problem remained unfeasible within and without the family who became worried and suddenly the unexpected happened.

On the seventh day, she spoke in Yoruba, asking to send for a man of God called Orimolade living in a given address in Lagos. According to her, this man was mandated to pray for her restoration to normalcy. Subsequently, Orimolade, who already knew through vision that such a request would be made received the emissary as they arrived, but felt reluctant to oblige, because it was raining at that time. A second request was made with the assurance from Abiodun that Orimolade would not be affected with the downpour of rain. Miraculously, the latter arrived at Abiodun's address dry, without any raincoat or umbrella for protection! That was another amazement to the family.

After this visitation, Abiodun was restored and resumed eating and drinking normally. Afterwards, she started to narrate her famous 'Celestial Visions'. This account outlined her celestial journeys with an angel friend, who showed her many wonders of heaven. The story of the Celestial Vision attracted known and unknown visitors to Saba Court, where she lived with her aunty, Mrs Comfort Moiett, wife of Superintendent General W. A. Hunnu-Moiett.

The increasing number of visitors nearly turned Saba Court to a Tourists Shrine, attracting an unpredictable number of visitors on a daily basis. The visitors' mission included listening to Abiodun's celestial vision stories and asking her for prayers for solution to various ailments and adversities. The fact that her aunty and husband were neither prepared nor equipped for hosting tourists to their premises, coupled with the fact that she could no longer perform her domestic and official duties as a 'Sales Girl' adequately prompted the suggestion that she should work with Orimolade as both of them have common callings and interests. The suggestion was mutually agreed between the Moietts and Orimolade and from there, an unplanned spiritual partnership was born. This partnership abruptly put an end to Orimolade's itinerancy as it became clear that more souls could be saved through a sedentary mission than Orimolade's itinerant alternative.

A Tale of Two Missions

Orimolade was already known as divinely ordained and empowered to confront idolatry, to preach the Gospel, to pray for deliverance and healing of the afflicted, to evangelise, to baptise converts. This he did with full commitment and enthusiasm on his itinerant mission. He saw this as a vocation and kept referring converts to different denominations. Due to his ability to showcase 'thaumaturgy' or 'wonderworking powers' throughout his ministry, he was dubbed the nickname of 'Baba Aladura' meaning, the father whose gifts include miracles and the efficacy of prayer. He most probably had no intention of remaining in Lagos as a final destination until Abiodun came into his life.

Abiodun on her part came from a different perspective. Her gifts emerged from the background of speaking in tongues, seeing visions, prophesying, evangelism and healing. As a young and attractive lady, she gained the admiration of many and based on this unique popularity, she was commissioned by Orimolade to lead evangelistic groups into the Yoruba heartlands including Ibadan, Abeokuta, Oke Ona, Effon Alaye, Ijebu and Ijesa lands. Her successful evangelical missions led to Orimolade conferring on her the title of 'Captain' in 1927.

The partnership of Orimolade and Abiodun is similar to the partnership between Adam and Eve, with the exception that the former partnership did not end up in marriage. God created Adam first but to make him complete in mission and evangelism, he created Eve to be his helper (Gen. 2:20). The mission of Adam and Eve was to:

Be fruitful, and multiply, and replenish the earth, and subdue it; and have dominion over the fish of the sea, and over the fowl of the air, and over every living thing that moveth upon the earth (Gen. 1:28).

Similarly, God called Orimolade first but since he was obsessed with itinerant ministry, He called Abiodun to serve as an anchor to the itinerancy. Since the divine partnership took shape, the Society stabilised into a sedentary ministry and naming ceremony and outline of doctrines followed.

The United Cherubim & Seraphim Society

Orimolade and Abiodun worked together successfully for four years from 1925 to 1929 with their gifts overlapping especially in the areas of preaching and healing. During 1925 the spiritual partnership and mission between the two peculiar giants grew to a level that prompted recognition and identity. It was suggested

Founders of Cherubim & Seraphim Church

to give the group a name. The search for a name was conducted through fasting and prayers.

The word 'Serafu'[66] was seen written in the clouds partly obscured in the sky and so the group was formally named as 'Egbe Serafu' in Yoruba, meaning, 'Seraphim Society' in August 1925. Again in March 1926, a female member dreamt of the second name. In her dream, it was suggested that 'Kerubu' (Cherubim) should be added because Cherubim and Seraphim are like twin angels in heaven and should not be separated. Subsequently, the Society was renamed as 'Egbe Kerubu ati Serafu' or 'Cherubim and Seraphim Society'.

At this juncture, the Cherubim & Seraphim started not as a church, but as a 'Society' or 'Band' of Christians from different denominations who believe in 'thaumaturgy' or Pentecostal charisma and the efficacy of prayers. Between 1925 to 1929 before the first schism in the Society, there was nobody known or called a 'Founder' and the group remained a Society or Band. Nobody held any titles except the two Leaders, Moses Orimolade popularly known and called 'Baba Aladura because of his peculiar and ethereal gifts; and Christiana Abiodun popularly known and called 'Captain', definitely earned and deserved the title as an energetic leader and an outstanding ambassador plenipotentiary of Cherubim & Seraphim everywhere she ministered.

At the beginning of the Society in 1925, Orimolade was about forty-six years old while Abiodun was about eighteen. In other words, Orimolade was a middle-aged man while Abiodun was a teenager. Even though there were members who were much older than both of them, it was the two that led the group with each

---

[66] As discerned by a learned local Anglican clergy in Lagos.

sitting on either side of the Altar Table after the Society became formalised. Besides, whenever the Society went on parades, which were common then in evangelism, it was the two Leaders only who were seated side by side in the carriage used, with everyone else following on foot.

GOD'S PLAN:

- *Harmony, united front, collective efforts, giant plans for extraordinary achievements.*

- *Unite competences to grow stronger and stronger, to the level of achieving great exploits.*

- *Promote the Gospel of Christ, ignoring earthly reward but expecting Divine blessings.*

- *Glorify God in daily thinking, speaking and actions.*

- *Seek after God's Kingdom and His righteousness without ceasing.*

- *Help others to achieve success and happiness at own personal inconvenience.*

- *Sacrifice own convenience to ensure happiness of others.*

- *Seek after the Kingdom of God and His righteousness.*

The Divided Cherubim and Seraphim Society

SATAN'S PLAN:

- *Stand Alone Syndrome, small and petty plans for short term gains.*

- *Divide and rule, fighting shy of attempting great exploits.*

- *Minimise propagation of the Gospel, prioritise personal benefits whilst opportunities last.*

- *Maximise personal glory at every opportunity in thinking, speaking and actions.*

- *Pretend to preach God's Kingdom while deceiving others to the contrary for personal gains.*

- *Explore dubious ways to harvest plenty with minimum efforts.*

- *Exploit others to reach maximum personal benefits and enjoy greater pleasures.*

- *Steal, kill and destroy in order to achieve personal ambitions.*

The unity and love shrouded the ministry until 1929 when unscrupulous members for their selfish ends set in to split the harmony between the two Leaders. The ugly 'Paul and Appolos' syndrome set in and the disharmony between the two became unmanageable between the two Leaders. Inevitably, two camps emerged with the membership split between them. Registration became imminent and in 1929, Captain Abiodun's group went with the name of

Cherubim & Seraphim Epistemology

'Cherubim & Seraphim Society' and was so registered. Another splinter group within Orimolade's camp gave him the ultimatum to effect reconciliation, failing which they would be forced to go their own way. The same group left Orimolade and registered as 'Praying Band of Cherubim & Seraphim' whilst the remaining loyal to Orimolade subsequently registered as 'The Eternal Sacred Order of Cherubim & Seraphim' on 1st February 1930.

The branches established through the evangelism of Captain Abiodun in the Western Region decided to distance themselves from splitting the Society further but resolved to remain neutral until the warring groups became reunited. Whilst the Praying Band appointed a Baba Aladura in parallel with Orimolade of the Eternal Sacred Order, the 'Western Conference' as the group outside Lagos were known, with their Headquarters in Ibadan decided to humbly address their Head as 'Alakoso' so as not to be seen as competing with Orimolade as 'Baba Aladura'.

Some Elders and members of the Western Conference (later known as 'Sacred Cherubim & Seraphim') worked for the Nigerian Railway and were transferred northwards to cities like Ilorin, Kaduna, Zaria, Kano etc. As it became not practicable to continue worshipping in the South, they eventually formed their own branch in the North and called it initially as 'C & S Church Movement, Northern Conference' and later as 'Holy Order of Cherubim & Seraphim Movement Church'. With the consent of Sacred C & S from Ibadan, they eventually appointed Nathaniel Coker as their first Baba Aladura in 1940.

The word 'Movement' in their name was actually meant to be perceived as 'Progressive' according to their Yoruba translation, which they called 'Kerubu ati Serafu Onitesiwaju'. At this point, sadly, Cherubim & Seraphim became a multi-headed church with five independent Heads. The multi-headedness was not intended to be permanent but as time went on, the different Sections gradually developed marked differentials in their liturgies and dress codes amongst others, although still bound by common doctrines and practices. With more splinter groups emerging and uncontrolled, the identity of Cherubim & Seraphim as a church has become fraught with challenges and repentance in humility has become imminent in order to repackage the profile and reputation of the church.

Notwithstanding that some ardent Members worked hard and prayed fervently for a reunited church with one Spiritual Head among the five groups, the hardliners in these groups remained adamant as they seemed to enjoy their independence in separatism.

They did not see the evil in separatism and chose to ignore the adage that 'united we stand, divided we fall' and that Jesus prayed for His disciples:

'that they may be one, as we are' (John 17:11).

The trend now, unfortunately, is growing worse as more and more 'leaders' especially from within the ranks of 'prophets' continue to split from each of the original five to claim the title of 'Baba Aladura'[67] and to run their groups in isolation. It is very doubtful if anyone will be willing to be called or to joyfully assume the position of 'Baba Aladura' today if the aspirants were required to drink from the same or similar cup, from which Orimolade drank!

---

[67] In C & S, the title of Baba Aladura is equivalent to GO (General Overseer) in Pentecostal churches.

- Like Jeremiah, he was sanctified from his mother's womb (Jer.1:5).

- He committed the whole of his life to mission, evangelism and kingdom exploits like John the Baptist.

- He lived a celibate life and had no taste for earthly possessions.

- He confidently confronted idolatry and pulled down pagan altars like Elijah.

- He boosted the membership of different denominations by referrals from his converts along the route of his missionary journey.

- He was humble and did not encourage being idolised. No ordination titles.

- He dedicated his whole life to God's mission without seeking earthly rewards.

It will be interesting to know how many past and present aspirants for high office in Cherubim & Seraphim can match Orimolade's profile or even get near to half way on the list! Unfortunately there has been a growing trend these days among some Elders in the C & S churches (as well as other denominations), to engage in unscrupulous struggles for power and positions, not as a desire to offer any reasonable contribution to promulgate the Gospel of Christ; but more often as unhealthy desire to boost personal ego, and worst still, to defraud and to turn Prayer Houses from worship venues into business centres, with undue emphasis on 'sowing seeds' and making money. However, Jesus taught that:

'man shall not live by bread alone, but by every word that proceeded from the mouth of God'(Matt. 4:4)

And,

'freely ye have received, freely give'(Matt. 10:8).

Compare Acts 8:18, where the love of money was the motivating factor for ministering as intended by Simon the pretender.

Who founded Cherubim & Seraphim Society?

The question may sound rather absurd but it definitely requires a measure of scrutiny particularly because it has become a matter of dispute especially after the 1929 split between Orimolade and Abiodun. When both worked together harmoniously for four years, the question did not arise. The word 'Founder' was neither used nor referred to at any time. Soon after the split, however, the question became prominent. A Yoruba proverb says 'Ija l'ode t'orin d'owe' meaning, 'it is disputes that breed contentious proverbs' It is reasonable to assume that the claim to Foundership might not have arisen from either of the Leaders themselves, but more likely from their arrogant supporters and misguided loyalists. Could it be that a song was spiritually composed through vision and prophecy by a prophet of the church to clarify that

'Jah Jehovah l'o d'Egbe yi sile, ki se ara'ye kan' meaning that *'Jah Jehovah established this Great Band (Church), not by any human initiative'*

The song was actually meant to throw light on some confusion as it began with

Cherubim & Seraphim Epistemology

'okunkun su, imole kan si tan, l'arin Egbe Seraf' meaning *'the darkness falls, and one great light shines forth, amidst the Seraphim'*

This is perhaps the greatest clue from the archives of the church to the question 'who founded Cherubim & Seraphim Society'

It has already been explained that Orimolade grew up to be an itinerary preacher and prophet with no desire to run any church and that the idea of a sedentary ministry did not arise until the involvement of Abiodun in 1925 as directed by the Holy Spirit. This means in other words that there was no such name as Cherubim & Seraphim associated with Orimolade prior to the spiritual partnership between the two leaders. A non-for-profit spiritual venture which neither of the leaders could even try to explain!

The argument that Abiodun was only a teenager in 1925 while Orimolade was a middle age, and as such, that Abiodun could not contend the leadership with Orimolade is not theologically valid, as God is no respecter of persons. In this argument, Abiodun stands at a double disadvantage culturally of being young and female. Both disadvantages were socially prejudiced in the environment in which both of them lived. But the work of God is never culturally nor socially limited. The Bible says:

'Out of the mouth of babes and sucklings God has ordained strength' (Ps.8:2).

God chose Moses and not his older and more fluent brother, Aaron; David was chosen over and above his older brothers; Joseph was tenth in line with his brothers but they all bowed down to him; the list can be endless. It is important to appreciate that Abiodun did not go to Orimolade as a patient in need of healing as many wrongly assume. Both of them came together with similar and overlapping spiritual gifts.

It is only reasonable to conclude that the bringing together of the two competences was of divine orientation and never of any human design. Their relationship is more than that of a 'father and a daughter' working together as in a family venture; but more of a fusion of distinct spiritual energies capable of reactivating thaumaturgy and ethereal gifts, which are the essential tools on which the church was founded at Pentecost for effective implementation of the church agenda. The purpose of the fusion of spiritual energies is principally for recruiting lost souls to populate the imminent kingdom of God to come, the new Jerusalem from heaven. This is the whole emphasis on which Cherubim & Seraphim Epistemology is being projected for the salvation of souls.

The Reunited Society

It came to a point when the leadership of Cherubim & Seraphim in their different contexts realised that the image of the church as perceived by the ecumenical community is less than originally intended as a respectable spiritual revival. Remedial actions became imminent, and restoration of the lost glory and dignity became urgent.

The church leadership, therefore, resolved to repent in humility, abandon multi-headed (and ugly) structure and return to a single headed church. The process of change therefore was put into action for full integration of the splinter groups of the church. The process has begun but not yet fully implemented. It is a joy to appreciate that presently, the ugly division that characterised Cherubim & Seraphim came to an end in 1986 with the coming together of all Sectional Heads and Elders who unanimously decided to elect a Supreme Head (Olori) who would co-ordinate the activities of the present Section Heads, mainly, the Baba Aladuras throughout the church. It was decided that succession process should be rotated initially between the original five Sections of the church viz:

- Eternal Sacred Order of Cherubim & Seraphim loyal to Orimolade,

- Cherubim & Seraphim Society loyal to Abiodun

- Praying Band of Cherubim & Seraphim ,

- Sacred Cherubim & Seraphim, and

- Holy Order of Cherubim & Seraphim Movement, in that order.

The first Supreme Head (Olori) should have been selected first from Eternal Sacred Order, but in consideration that the Co-Founder (otherwise called the Living Founder at that time) was still alive, it was resolved to honour her with the privilege of being the first to be so installed. Hence, Her Eminence Captain Mother Prophetess Christiana Abiodun Emmanuel was enthroned as the First Supreme Head (Olori) in 1986. At her demise in 1994, the title reverted to the first church, the Eternal Sacred Order, when their Baba Aladura, Amos Afolabi Ogunkunle was enthroned as the second Supreme Head (Olori) 1996-2004. The third Supreme Head went to Baba Aladura Abel Olujimi Akinsanya of the Praying Band of Cherubim & Seraphim. He reigned from 2006-2014. The fourth Supreme Head (Olori), His Most Eminence, Prophet Dr Solomon Adegboyega Alao of the Sacred Cherubim and Seraphim ascended the throne from 2015 to date.

Founders of Cherubim & Seraphim Church

The current Constitutional Review now stipulates that the rotation of the title of Supreme Head (Olori) should go round the first five Sectional Heads once only, after which a permanent holder would be elected by all Seraphs. The last on the rotation would be from the Holy Order of Cherubim & Seraphim Movement Church. The 'Reunited' Cherubim & Seraphim Church is now moving on from the position of disintegration to a strong and united church which through the power of the Holy Spirit will effectively promulgate the Gospel of Christ and win more souls for His soon coming Kingdom.

CHAPTER 7

DOCTRINES AND DOCTRINAL FORMATIONS

It should be recognised that 'Doctrines' are not strictly biblical but man made. They are statements designed for believers to be studied and put into practice by adherents. They can be dangerous to believers as they tend to be dogmatic in their attitudes to religion. They are the root of most schisms in the church as church leaders grow to understand aspects of scripture differently. Differentiated doctrines contribute to wrecking church unity than contributing to build it. Doctrines can be seen as Mission Statements of new churches, which make them different to the others. So, whenever a new church is formed, people ask to know their doctrinal statement in order to discover their true identity. Most AIC churches on inauguration do not start by outlining their doctrines. Now, let us examine the development of Doctrines in the Cherubim & Seraphim.

The Original Five Doctrinal Statements of C & S

The Orimolade Constitution of 1925 was very brief in outlining the C & S Doctrines. The following were stated:

1. The Order holds unshaken faith in the Holy Bible as the Word of God and in Salvation through Jesus Christ, and in the Trinity in Unity, the use of Incense, purification by prayer and fasting and the resurrection of the dead.

Doctrines and Doctrinal Formations

2. Its first and primary work is that of prayer and the PREACHING OF THE GOSPEL.

3. It believes in the curative effect of prayer for all afflictions, spiritual and temporal, but condemns and abhors the use of charms or fetish, witchcrafts or Sorcery of any kind and all heathenish sacrifices and practices.

4. It is not averse to the judicious use of curative herbs, the engagement of qualified medical practitioners of doctors or the use of patent medicines or other drugs.

5. It endorses and does practise the sanctification of water by prayer and the effect of such consecrated or holy water for every purpose.

The above statement of doctrine was included in Orimolade's Constitution published by the Eternal Sacred Order of the Cherubim & Seraphim (founded in 1925 and incorporated in 1930) and registered by Charles A Gordon, Registrar of Companies in Lagos and dated 1st February, 1930.[68]

These were stated in the light of knowledge and belief at that time. It is interesting to know that the church was not founded on the ground of doctrinal differences from any other church. Matters of doctrine were of little importance and matters of prayers for deliverance and healing were of paramount importance at the inception of the church.

No doctrinal statement was made, therefore, prior to registration in 1930. It is presumed that the above five statements were made in answer to the question of the Registrar of Companies upon

---

[68] Certificate No.316, The Register of Companies, Lagos 1930

application to register. In other words, doctrinal matters or statements to the Cherubim & Seraphim (like with other AICs), are supplementary rather than primary to the ministry of the church; an afterthought perhaps!

The Tabula Rasa Approach

Like many AICs, the Cherubim & Seraphim was not built on a predetermined set of doctrines. As the church grew and developed, it became unavoidable to remain without a set of doctrines. Just like the Hebrew history started with their knowledge of God as Jehovah Sabaoth in Exodus, and the Genesis stories including the Creation Story came later as an addition to their history; so, the Cherubim & Seraphim Doctrines (like many other AICs) were developed only after the church had been in existence for some years. The development of the statement of doctrines, therefore, got started in a little way and has been developing ever since to reflect the ethos of the church in her growth to adulthood and maturity. The development also essentially gives answers to questions that are often asked about the beliefs of the church. Undoubtedly, the doctrinal statements will continue to expand in light of developments in the future coupled with external factors that may impinge on the life of the church.

Some attempts have been made by various factions of the church to compile a coherent set of beliefs but yet it has not been possible to arrive at a consensus about any set that is acceptable to all the factions. However, during the mid 1980s, some development was attempted by the Cherubim & Seraphim Council of Churches Worldwide to outline what was called 'Tenets of Faith.'[69]

---

[69] Fakeye, G O & Fabiyi, E A, *TENETS OF FAITH for C & S Council of Churches Worldwide,* Supreme Press Limited, Lagos, 1990

Twenty-seven statements were made under the headings of: God, God the Father, The Son, The Holy Spirit, The Holy Bible, The Three Creeds, God's Creation and Providence, Man and his sin, Salvation by grace through faith, The Holy Spirit and the Christian life, The Church of Christ, Discipline, Ceremonies and Practices, The Church and Healing, The Mission of the Church to Society, The Minister of the Church, Christian Baptism, The Lord's Supper, Symbols of Christian Brotherhood, Symbols of Christian Order, Marriage and the Home, Discipleship and non-conformity, Christian Integrity, Love and non-Resistance, The Christian and the State, The Final Consummation and Seven Pillars. This latest development nearly equalled the Thirty-nine Articles of Faith of the Anglican Communion.

Implied Doctrinal Statements

Preamble

Unlike the doctrines of most churches, especially the Protestant Churches which commenced as a result of protest or disagreement on some aspects of their parent church, the Cherubim & Seraphim doctrines and beliefs have taken the evolution route. That is because, the C & S emerged as a 'Society' or 'Band' before becoming a 'Church'. The emergence was not the result of schism from any parent church or any denomination.

It is worthy of note that all aspects of our doctrines and beliefs are Biblically grounded. The alternative to Bible reference is inspired prophecy and spiritual revelation. Both visions and revelations were the result of prayers and fasting by members during the formative period of the Church. The following, therefore, are the evolved statements of doctrine:

The Bible

We believe in both the Old and the New Testaments as a true account of God's Words to help humanity in breaking down barriers between us and the love of God; and to build bridges across the gulf which Satan developed between God and humanity. We believe that the New Testament is the fulfilment of the Old Testament prophecy and the improvement on its theology. We believe in the imminence of the Rapture and the establishment of Christ's Kingdom on earth. Our theology is therefore closely linked to the Apocalyptic prophecies and the end-time signs of the coming Kingdom. Adherents are therefore prepared and groomed to accept Christ on His coming again, when all governments in the world will have to surrender to the rule of Christ.

The Trinity

We believe in the Godhead, the Father, Son & Holy Spirit (one in three and three in one) as affirmed in the Hebrew Scripture (Deu.6:4) *'Hear, O Israel. The Lord our God is one Lord.'* One of the titles of God is Lord. As all Christians agree that Jesus is Lord also, he is Lord indeed, not apart from the Father, but as part of the Godhead because God will not share His glory with anyone (Isa 42:8). God is omnipotent and is capable of manifesting Himself in different forms, not least as Father or Son or the Holy Spirit. Even beyond that God appeared for example, to Jacob as a man when He wrestled with him overnight and changed his name from Jacob to Israel before blessing him (Gen.32:30).

The Creeds

We believe in the three Creeds composed by Church Councils during the first centuries. We recite the Apostles' Creed in every Sunday liturgy and the Nicene Creed whenever we celebrate the Holy Communion. The Athanasian Creed is rarely used although we have no objection to its contents except for the negative expression of damnation for those who fail to adhere to its assertions. Such negativity seems to ignore the power of atonement in the blood of Christ.

The Sacraments

We believe in and practise the two principal sacraments in the life of Jesus, namely: Baptism and |Holy Communion. All other rituals, counted as sacraments by many other denominations like anointing with the oil, sprinkling of water, Holy Matrimony and funerals are all important 'Sacramentals' which we observe and cherish in Cherubim & Seraphim Epistemology.

We believe in the baptism of believers (minimum age of twelve years, at which age, Jesus was engaged in meaningful dialogue with learned authorities in the Temple) by total immersion in water thrice in the name of the Father, and of the Son, and of the Holy Spirit (being the Trinitarian tradition). We do not baptise infants ,but we do practise the ritual of 'Christening' using three elements of water, salt and honey (with a little of each being put in the mouth of the babe with pronouncements and blessings at each time) and we believe that this ritual is as valid for salvation as water baptism.

We believe in celebrating the Holy Communion at important occasions like at baptism and ordination; at special other occasions as a congregation deems fit. Some congregations do regularise the celebration like celebrating on a monthly basis. In the celebrations, we believe that the bread and wine that we share are transformed into the body and blood of Christ. Therefore, we take the celebration seriously and regard it as sacred.

Water Consecration

We believe that the spirit of God works wonders through the medium of water. Psalm 29:3 teaches us that *'The voice of the Lord is upon the waters, the God of glory thundereth, the Lord is upon many waters.'* We believe that the spirit of the Lord which descended healing power into the pool of Bethsaida, the pool of Siloam and the River Jordan can also descend into our bottles of water when we present them for consecration.

Transubstantiation

This concept is fundamental to our doctrine and beliefs. It is the cornerstone of our faith in God. Hebrew 11:1 describes faith as 'the substance of things hoped for, the evidence of things not seen' Transubstantiation is built on faith. Academic theology teaches detailed analysis of Scripture but does not teach on matters relating to faith! In Luke 17:5,

'the apostles said unto the Lord, 'increase our faith. And the Lord said 'if ye had faith as a grain of mustard seed, ye might say unto this sycamine tree, be thou plucked up by the root, and be thou planted in the sea, and it should obey you.'

With this kind of mindset, therefore, we believe that transubstantiation or the change of the substance of elements we present for consecration can work wonders. We take the Holy Communion seriously and believe that the elements we use are being transformed to receive power for sanctification of our bodies and souls. Similarly, we believe that our consecrated water is essentially transformed into spiritual medication for different purposes of deliverance, healing, breakthrough and upliftment. As we use them, we believe that ordinariness is taken away from the water and is replaced with power for the efficacy of prayer.

Priesthood of Believers

We believe that all members who are spiritually gifted have a part to play in our Prayer House as James urges believers to *'be doers of the word, and not hearers only . . .'* Wonderfully, most adherents embrace the enthusiasm and learn through Sunday Schools and external Bible sessions to uplift their knowledge of Scripture and to exercise their God-given gifts and work for the propagation of the Gospel of Christ. Many such gifted members are subsequently invited for ordination to appropriate grades in our hierarchy.

Concept of Salvation

We believe that salvation of individuals rests with God and that neither faith nor work can justify any believer at the time of judgement. The Epistle of James chapter 2 outlines the pros and cons of justification. If dependent on faith alone, then there will be undue complacency. If on the other hand, the dependency is on works, then there is the danger of hypocrisy as in the story Jesus narrated about the Pharisee and the Publican in Luke 18:10-14. Apart from the reliance on faith and works, the mercy of God is paramount as He said to Moses: *'I will show mercy unto whom I will show mercy.' (Ex 33:19).*

Predestination & Election

We believe that God has a specific purpose for all His creations. individuals and races. Examples of this in the Old Testament include the conception, birth and life of Esau and Jacob as narrated in Genesis Chapters 27—35. Also, the story of Joseph is a glaring illustration of the purpose of God. It can also be said that the conception, birth, life, death and resurrection of Jesus were being predetermined by divine will.

Romans 8: 28-30 specifically tells us about those:

who are called according to his purpose. For whom he did foreknow, he also did predestinate to be conformed to the image of his Son, that he might be the firstborn among many brethren. Moreover, whom he did predestinate, them he also called, and whom he called, them he also justified, and whom he justified, them he also glorified.

Talking about his predetermined death, Jesus said to his disciples:

'The Son of man goeth as it is written of him, but woe unto that man by whom the Son of man is betrayed!' (Matt.26:24).

Supernatural Powers

We believe like other 'white robed churches' that there are invisible powers that impact on our lives. The belief has nothing to do with ancestor worship as it is commonly assumed by other Christians, but shows higher powers over and above human powers created by

God. Some of them can be good and some bad. We believe that the good ones are angels of God and the bad ones, angels of Satan but all created by God.

Whenever supernatural powers are mentioned, some Christians become nervous as they do not believe in their existence. As Prayer Warriors, therefore, we learn to fight against the angels of Satan which are capable of inflicting evil on men. In the New Testament, Paul affirms these powers as

'principalities, powers, rulers of the darkness of this world and spiritual wickedness in high places.' (Eph 6:12).

Against these, the vigilant Prayer Warriors must vigorously fight, and with fortitude, report victory in the name of Christ. The fighting or war against these adverse forces is not by deploying weapons of mass destruction, but by resorting to prayers in faith and with fasting, believing that the heavenly hosts will take over the battle and win.

Unknown to us, God in His wrath can also inflict evil on men through His great army in the form of 'locust, cankerworm, caterpillar and the palmerworm' (Joel 2:25). With this kind of mindset, we believe that men can suffer from th e wickedness of Satan and his angels; as well as from the anger of God in punishment for our wrongdoings. Other beliefs and practices are drawn from Semitic and African cultures. Such practices as:

Robing in white at worship

Members being robed in white is essentially a spiritual privilege, in imitation of the heavenly saints. Being robed in white has been described as an image of forgiveness and redemption. White robes worn by Cherubim & Seraphim in worship are not simply another kind of social dress. They are consecrated and hence a reminder to the wearer that their thoughts and conduct are to be Christ-like as they embark on the worship of God and exercise spiritual powers. That is why our white prayer gowns are presented before qualified Elders upon acquisition, to be consecrated before being worn. Thereafter, the prayer gowns can be worn in worship in the Prayer House as well as at home or elsewhere for efficacy of prayers. They symbolise God's forgiveness, sanctification and redemption as well as deliverance and healing. Wearing the prayer gown makes the prayer warrior feel like putting on the whole armour of God, with which failure is not an option, and victory is an imperative.

The C&S has identified with the apocalypse tradition and culture from inception. The Founder of the Cherubim & Seraphim, Saint Moses Orimolade Tunolase did prescribe that Members should be robed in white for worship of the Almighty God. The tradition implies that earthly saints should be robed in white. John, the author of the Book of Revelation has described how heavenly saints are robed in white. They have to be so robed to appear before the throne of God and to worship Him in the beauty of His holiness. A particular worship song goes:

> *John saw them coming, John saw them coming*
> *John saw them coming, robed in white*
> *They all were numbered, they all were numbered*
> *They all were numbered, robed in white.*

We should be asking what exactly is the significance of the White Robes of the Heavenly Saints? It is simply an image of forgiveness and redemption. The hosts of heaven, therefore, are the blessed of the Lord, *'whose transgressions are forgiven and whose sins are covered'. (Ps.32:1)*. They are washed by the blood of Jesus, redeemed and brought into the heavenly Kingdom. The white robed Cherubim & Seraphim symbolise their representatives on earth who aspire to worship God on earth, *'as it is in heaven' (Matt.6:10)*.

The Cherubim & Seraphim worship could be described as a foretaste of the endtime worship in the impending Rapture of our Lord. The redeemed of the Lord will essentially be robed in white as described above. The seventh chapter of the Book of Revelation throws greater light of the hitherto elusive Rapture. The privileged who will robe in white at the arrival of the Lamb of God will be selected. That is why the above song says that 'they all were numbered'. There is a criteria for inclusion of the number. Verse 13 of this chapter asked the question:

What are these which are arrayed in white robes? And whence came they?

The answer came in verses 14 & 15:

These are they which came out of great tribulation, and have washed their robes, and made them white in the blood of the Lamb. Therefore, are they before the throne of God, and serve Him day and night in His temple; and He that sitteth on the throne shall dwell among them.

'shall dwell among them' is a special privilege. It echoes the reign of God as described in Psalms 80:1 & 99:1 *'He sitteth between the Cherubim'* wherefore the people must tremble and the earth must move! With the confidence that God dwells in the midst of us, the challenges that lie ahead of Members are more than halfway solved. Total solution will depend on the level of faith and prayer accompanying our request. That being said, it should be

recognised that no one can boast of an absolute solution to any problem. The believer is expected to take the request to the Lord and leave it there. The Holy Spirit takes over and dispenses the solution.

Some critics question the idea of mass robing in white in worship. In the Anglo-Catholic tradition, only the clergy and choir are so robed. Why then is mass robing in white in the Cherubim and Seraphim? The simple answer is that it is like an outward sign of being born again, which every member is called to be. It is also reflecting uniformity as Jesus was with his disciples to identify with them (see more in the next section). The song below almost makes it mandatory to be robed in white before worship. It makes sound that being so robed is a delight of God. That being so, it then amounts to a special privilege to be robed in white for worship.

> *Have you been to Jesus for the cleansing power?*
> *Are you washed in the blood of the Lamb?*
> *Are you fully truly trusting in His grace this hour?*
> *Are you washed in the blood of the Lamb?*
> *Chorus: Are you washed ... in the blood*
> *In the soul cleansing blood of the Lamb?*
> **Are your garments spotless, are they white as snow?**
> *Are you washed in the blood of the Lamb?*

Members of the C&S are preparing to proclaim the acceptable year of the Lord when earthly Cherubim and Seraphim are identified with the heavenly ones by robing in white, thus declaring that they have given their life to Christ and singing the praise of the

Almighty God. That in essence makes the C&S particularly proud to be seen as:

'a chosen generation, a royal priesthood, an holy nation, a peculiar people, that you should shew forth the praises of him who has called you out of darkness into his marvellous light' (I Peter 2: 9).

'a chosen generation' implies that *'many are called, but a few are chosen' (Matt. 22:14).*

If therefore, you have been counted among the chosen, why deny Him who chose you? Jesus did warn that:

Whosoever shall deny me before men, him will I also deny before my Father which is in heaven (Matt. 10:33)

Robing in white is symbolic of the preparation for the second coming of Christ. It signifies readiness as a bride (the church is the bride and Christ, the bridegroom).

It may be more convenient to name the White Prayer Gown a Bridal Gown. That is how it is described in the Book of Revelation.

Let us be glad and rejoice and give honour to him; for the marriage of the Lamb is come, and his wife hath made herself ready. And to her was granted that she should be arrayed in fine linen, clean and white; for the fine linen is the righteousness of saints (Rev. 19: 7/8).

It is with this rejoicing that we can rightly sing the song:

> *My friend what happens to you, to become Cherubim,*
> *My friend what happens to you, to become Seraphim?*
> *Jesus called, I answered, if you like, you can come with me;*

Cherubim & Seraphim Epistemology

Jesus called, I answered, if you like, you can come with me.

The simple conclusion on white robing culture is that those who understand its significance in terms of renewing their focus on the personal and corporate requirements for the seconding coming of Christ: (i) their personal journey for their souls to become white as snow and Christ-like; (ii) the church responsibility to be free from blemishes and to discharge kingdom work and be the salt of the earth for transformational change; should continue to celebrate the habit because of the spiritual benefits as outlined above, amongst others. A popular songs goes:

> *Feel alright, no condemnation, feel alright*
> *No condemnation, no condemnation in my soul.*
> *In my soul today, in my soul today;*
> *Jesus washed all my sins away,*
> *In my soul today, in my soul today,*
> *No condemnation in my soul.*

Whilst outsiders may not easily distinguish the outer wear from other white garment churches, the character, conduct and integrity of the C&S church should aim to reflect the character of Christ and standing on biblical truths transform its environment, so that people will ask 'Which God do you serve'.

Uniformity

Uniformity is ensured when all members are robed in white. Then there can be no room for confusion. Jesus and his disciples were robed in white. They always look alike. That is why Judas had to identify him by kissing before his arrest by the Jewish authorities, as they were confused as to which one was Jesus. Uniformity is therefore important to the idea of robing in white. it promotes solidarity and obliterates differentiation. His disciples were robed in white and because he wanted to 'be in the midst of them' he too was robed in white in order to identify with them.

This kind of solidarity is common in the African and Semitic culture, and which can be strange to other cultures as is the parable of Jesus on wedding invitations and the need to be dressed in the wedding uniform. (in Yoruba language, this is described as 'Aso Ebi' which is still in practice today but without the strict rule of exclusion).

'And when the king came in to see the guests, he saw there a man which had not on a wedding garment: And he saith unto him, Friend, how camest thou in hither not having a wedding garment? And he was speechless . . . ' (Matt.22:11-13).

In Africa and particularly in Nigeria, special dresses are always prescribed for guests to weddings, funerals, birthday ceremonies amongst other celebrations. When, as it often happens some people turn up at such gatherings without the prescribed uniforms (usually referred to in Yoruba language as 'Aso Ebi') they constitute embarrassment and look like 'Uninvited Guests' Perhaps from this cultural background, it can be understood why the Cherubim & Seraphim and other 'white garment' churches would like their adherents to be robed in white in worship. This is in addition to other reasons including that the uniformity facilitates oneness and harmony; eliminating the incidence of distraction in worship when those who are from affluence backgrounds can come in to worship in a sort of 'Joseph's coats' which, apart from being a distraction, it can also create unnecessary envy for other worshippers who cannot afford such outfits.

More importantly, robing in white is the Biblical culture of the heavenly Cherubim and Seraphim (Rev. 7:13). As this scripture teaches, it is a privilege for saints to robe in white and rather than be ashamed of it, the 'white garment' Christians should be proud of the fact that they are practising on earth, what the saints are doing in heaven. A convenient literal meaning can be found in the Gospels. The Lord's Prayer says

'Thy will be done on earth, as it is in heaven.' (Matt.6:10)

Instances like these can only point to the need for Christians from all cultures to liaise with one another in dialogue for mutual understanding of the richness in the variety of the word of God. Inter-cultural dialogue and sharing of competences can, therefore, become powerful tools that are necessary to enrich our knowledge and love of God.

Divine presence

- It is important to stress the assurance of divine presence when believers are

- in one accord and not in disarray

- in unity and not in disunity

- in harmony and not in disharmony

- in love and not in hatred

- in believing and not in disbelief

- in readiness to serve and not in expecting to be served

- in humility like Isaiah's self condemnation and receiving mercy; and not

- in arrogance like Jonah's arguments and self justification.

All the above amongst others, certainly attract divine presence at no cost to the believer. Divine presence breeds unmerited blessings in good health, long life and prosperity. It is quite possible to invite divine presence to one's life but the experience is not very common these days as it should be. Let us examine what the Scripture is saying about personal sanctity that is conducive to divine presence.

Who shall ascend into the hill of the Lord? Or who shall stand in his holy place? He that hath clean hands and a pure heart, who hath not lifted up his soul unto vanity nor sworn deceitfully. He shall receive the blessing from the Lord, and righteousness from the God of his salvation (Ps.24:3-5)

These criteria can be difficult to fulfil as human beings. It is only a few who completely surrender their lives to Christ that could come near, only near the fulfilment. There are some who feel so complacent that they think you do not have to attempt living a holy life because it is difficult and more so, that Jesus has taken the burden off our shoulders by his sacrifice on the cross. But Paul reminded us:

Shall we continue in sin, that grace may abound? (Rom. 6:1)

It is quite clear that God cannot live with sin because light and darkness cannot live together. That is why no human can see God and live. Jesus could only communicate with humans because he is God incarnate. Without the human embodiment of God, Jesus as one in three and three in one would not be able to articulate with humans as God is a consuming fire!

That is why God demands sanctity of the believer in preparation to 'ascend into the hill of the Lord' He has used the personal sanctity on the Sabbath to illustrate the need for holiness before divine presence and blessing can be bestowed:

If thou turn away thy foot from the Sabbath, from doing thy pleasure on my holy day; and call the Sabbath a delight, the holy of the Lord, honourable; and shall honour him, not doing thine own ways, nor finding thine own ways, nor finding thine own pleasure, nor speaking thine own words: then shall thou delight thyself in the Lord; and I will cause thee to ride upon the high places of the earth, and feed thee with the heritage of Jacob thy father; for the mouth of the Lord hath spoken it. (Isa.58:13/14).

The Sabbath was intended to be dedicated in time, function and celebration to the LORD to recall His great creation (Gen 2:1-3, Ex 20:11) and His saving grace (Ex 31:12-17). Not to follow secular interests, sensual desires, or idle talk, but rather honouring God by focusing on spiritual matters and divine worship.

The sanctity of our Prayer Houses

From inception, any building acquired by Cherubim & Seraphim Churches for the purpose of worship is regarded as 'Sanctum Sanctorum' meaning 'holy of holies' which generally refers in Latin texts to the holiest place of the Ancient Israelites, inside the Tabernacle, and later in the Jewish Temple in Jerusalem where the Ark of Covenant was kept. Access to the holy of holies (which was veiled by curtains) was limited to the Priests and High Priests in

Judaism. However, at the last breath of Christ on the cross, and at the pronouncement of the last word *'Father, into Thy hand I commit my spirit'*

'the veil of the temple was rent in the midst' (Lk 23:45)

By theological interpretation, the exclusiveness of the 'Sanctorum' was broken as 'the veil of the temple was rent in the midst' but the sanctity of the Temple remains as Jesus did remind the people that

'My house shall be called the house of prayer; but ye have made it a den of thieves' (Matt.21:13).

Consequently,

He went into the temple of God, and cast out all them that sold and bought in the temple, and overthrew the tables of the moneychangers, and the seats of them that sold doves. (Matt.21:12)

It is needless to say that we need Jesus to visit our Prayer Houses today to exercise similar cleansing; and to restore sanctity in our places of worship, because it is now difficult to distinguish between a Prayer House and a Business Centre. Many Pastors and Prophets have turned into Business Gurus to the detriment of propagating the Gospel of Christ!

Apart from the command of God for Moses to

Draw not nigh hither; put off thy shoes from off thy feet, for the place whereon thou standest is holy ground. (Ex.3:5)

Cherubim & Seraphim Epistemology

And also to Joshua who encountered a similar experience of articulating with holiness as he met the Captain of the host of the Lord who commanded him to

Loose thy shoe from off thy foot; for the place whereon thou standest is holy. (Jos 5:15).

These commands clearly point to the fact that wherever the presence of the Lord is envisaged, there must essentially be a good measure of holiness accompanying. Holiness requires both spiritual and physical attention to cleanliness. This is why the Pharisees (like the Muslims) wash their face, hands and feet before prayers; and they remove their shoes before entering their places of worship. The physical washing acts do help to remind the worshipper of the necessity to also repent and wash the heart to be acceptable to God. The observance serves as a constant reminder that God always requires holiness in articulating with men. Such outward cleanliness is also synonymous to baptism by water as a symbol of repentance and conversion. The observance of baptism by immersion, certainly forms part of the contributing factors leading to any claim towards efficacy of prayers in the C & S epistemology.

Holiness requires cleanliness in both its inward and outward formats. Holiness envelops God's presence at all times. Around the throne of God in heaven, the Cherubim and Seraphim in His presence are consumed with holiness as they continually sing Holy, holy, holy is the Lord of hosts: the whole earth is full of his glory. (Isaiah. 6:3). Removing of shoes is part of the outward format of humility and honouring the presence of God. When God sees our hearts sincerely humbled before Him, seeking to return to His standards, He is merciful and gracious to remove our guilt and to commission us to move forward in His service.

Doctrines and Doctrinal Formations

In the older C&S parishes, there were always apartments called 'Shiloh' where sick patients are admitted into residence for a period of time, pending recovery; just like hospital admissions for treatment. The Prayer House itself is another 'Shiloh' which is open everyday and possibly in some cases, every hour with at least a Priest or Prophet, in attendance to minister to visitors. It was such a visit that brought blessing to Hannah as she brought her personal anguish to God in silent prayer. She needed a God who is charged with enormous power to turn her fortune around. She found a God who is capable of transforming her predicament into joy. She was blessed with the provision of a son according to her request. She gave birth to Samuel, whom she dedicated to the service of God in the Temple.

In Shiloh, consecrated water and olive oil, coupled with prayer and fasting by Elders replace medical and/or herbal prescriptions for the duration of admission. Such admissions invariably help the patients to close their eyes to domestic chores and to focus on receiving divine healing or deliverance. One of the beneficiaries of Shiloh ministry remarked that Shiloh was not a church, but a hospital where, whatever goes wrong can always be put right by the power that is above all powers on earth and in heaven.

The above kind of observances are employed and in most cases, speedy recoveries are recorded and wonderful testimonies are consequently given during church Services. Sometimes, spiritual directives in the form of visions and revelations are given as to what kind of songs and/or scriptures to be applied; why such are appropriate; when the prayers are to be said; where they should be said; how they should be said and who should officiate in such prayers. The Holy Spirit is the driver in this discourse; and spiritual directives differ from case to case. This is why in the C&S

dispensation, no one can be judgemental about physical cleanliness of any officiating elder or Prayer Warrior. The Holy Spirit is always in control. C&S is probably the closest Christian denomination to Judaism in terms of the sanctity of church buildings. As a result, no shoes, dead bodies/blood or any other abominations are allowed inside the worship areas of the buildings.

Clapping and dancing

Most songs and choruses are usually accompanied with good music, clapping and dancing during Divine Services and Prayer Meetings. The introduction of drumming for music in addition to organ/piano music in worship was started by the Cherubim & Seraphim in Nigeria. At the beginning the idea, which triggered clapping, dancing and raising up hands, was branded an anathema by other Christian denominations which were at the forefront of Christian mission to the country. They reacted as if there was no biblical basis or precedent to the new ideas. But after several decades of the growth of C&S and after the older established mission churches started losing members to the church; this idea of clapping, dancing and raising up hands in worship became popular; and now in Nigeria, it is difficult to distinguish between worship patterns across denominational divides. Clapping and dancing in worship can rightly be seen as expressions of joy and praise to the Almighty God for His mercy and blessings.

O clap your hands, all ye people; shout unto God with the voice of triumph (Ps.47:1).

Let the floods clap their hands: let the hills be joyful together (Ps. 98:8)

For you shall go out with joy, and be led forth with peace; the mountains and the hills shall break forth before you with singing, and all the trees of the field shall clap their hands (Is.55:12)

The quotations as above, incidentally, are all from the Old Testament. There is no evidence of clapping and dancing during worship in the New Testament. But it cannot be argued that the C&S or indeed, the AIC necessarily have introduced African culture into Christianity. These practices are common in Judaism from their Semitic culture. It is already argued that both African and Semitic cultures are similar if not one and the same. Hence, the similarities in worship between Judaism and AIC.

CHAPTER 8

MODE OF MINISTRY

For 1500 years, the Western church has encouraged church leadership in terms of Teachers and Pastors as being sufficient for the ministry. The other three outlined by Paul in his letter to the Ephesians namely, Evangelists, Prophets and Apostles have been regarded as no longer relevant and hence, marginalised. The Cherubim & Seraphim has brought these ministries back into active participation in 'the perfecting of the ministry of Christ'.

The Ephesian 5-Hierarchy Ministry

The restoration of the latter may have been perfect, if only sufficient care has been exercised in the recruitment process. Historically, it has transpired that the opposite is true in many, if not most of the independent congregations. Inexperienced and ungifted people have, in many cases, found their way to the hierarchies due to egoism, favouritism and nepotism. The result has always been inefficient ministry that is contrary to the wishes of Christ and unhealthy to the church. Where there is such careless or prejudiced recruitment, there can only be an inefficient system of ministry which gives a negative impression to analysts who would be apt to ask *'Can there any good thing come out of Nazareth?.* But to this old question, Philip answered *'Come and see.' (John 1:46).* The same answer is appropriate to the sceptics who only look at the insignificant number of dysfunctional players rather than look to the spiritual enrichment and practical Christianity provided by the genuine AIC as a whole.

Mode of Ministry

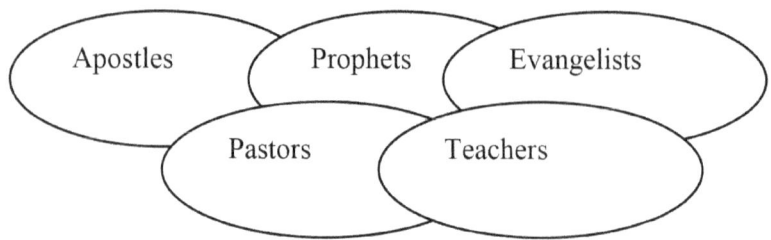

5-Hierarchy Mode of Ministry in the C & S

Ministry adaptation in the Cherubim & Seraphim Church derives primarily from the Ephesian model as outlined by Paul the Apostle. Ephesians 4:12 describes the offices of the Apostles, Prophets, Evangelists, Pastors and Teachers as necessary

'for the perfecting of the saints, for the work of the ministry, for the edifying of the body of Christ.'

This model is essentially hierarchical as understood in C & S, as there is hierarchy within the heavenly bodies. So the C & S as a white garment church, representing the angels on earth, are also hierarchical. Romans 1:1 says 'Let every soul be subject unto the higher powers.' By implication in the C & S, therefore, Teachers are subject to Pastors, who in turn are subject to Evangelists; Evangelists to Prophets and Prophets also subject to Apostles. This simply means that the higher authority occupies mentorship through motivation by giving instructions or directives to the lower hierarchy, but with humility and intent on perfecting the ministry of Christ.

These hierarchical powers have merits and demerits. The merits include the passing down of knowledge and experience from top to bottom. It is a relationship similar to that between Moses and

Joshua or between Elijah and Elisha in the Old Testament and between Paul and Timothy or Titus in the New. It is in conformity with the Fifth Commandment given to Moses:

'Honour thy father and thy mother: that thy days may be long upon the land which the Lord thy God giveth thee' (Exodus 20:12).

The demerits include the clamour for power of some members who unscrupulously aspire to reach the top hierarchy with or without adequate training and aptitude for the positions. This kind of ambition is not a sin in itself (although it can be described as covetousness as per Ex. 20:17). It can be a blessing if the aspirant works hard to fulfil the demands of the office desired and is guided by the Holy Spirit. On the other hand, it can be a failure and disaster if the aspirant has not the necessary gifting, knowledge, experience and integrity to fulfil the demands of the office. Saint Paul explains to Timothy and Titus thus:

'If a man desire the office of a bishop, he desireth a good work. A bishop then must be blameless, the husband of one wife, vigilant, sober, of good behaviour, given to hospitality, apt to teach; not given to wine, no striker, not greedy of filthy lucre, but patient, not a brawler, not covetous; one that ruleth well his own house, having his children in subjection with all gravity; for if a man knows not how to rule his own house, how shall he take care of the church of God? (I Timothy 3:1-13 & Titus 1: 7-9).

For all aspirants for high office in the church, adherence to these criteria is the first step. Even when an officer is already ordained into a high office and there is evidence of violation of the criteria, such an officer should be asked to step down in honour in order to preserve the integrity of the office. It is better to step down in

Mode of Ministry

honour and humility and be saved, than to cling to office in defiance and be damned.

Despite the hierarchical stance as outlined above, there are certain proponents of the egalitarian perspective of the Ephesian model of ministry. This perspective asserts that all the various offices of Teachers, Pastors, Evangelists, Prophets and Apostles should all be at parity in status and none should be seen as superior to the other. Whatever the office, therefore, it would be simply a matter of specialisation. Hence, those who specialise in teaching should be anointed as Teachers, and never to be moved to another office as in promotion from lower to higher. Such proponents in the C & S are in the minority and their innovative ideas are genuinely aimed at eradicating superiority syndromes among ministers. Relationships between the five hierarchies in this egalitarian perspective, therefore, are rather more horizontal than vertical. Perhaps there can be movements sideways as occasioned by shifts in gifts and specialisation; but not as in a promotion or demotion scenario.

It is interesting to note that most denominations have hierarchical ministry while only a few prefer to be egalitarian. The Quakers or Society of Friends are examples of the latter scenario; whilst the Salvation Army are not only hierarchical but also military in their ministry. The Quakers would rather call you by your first name and are reluctant to append Mr, Mrs, Miss, Reverend, Doctor, Professor, Pastor, Bishop or any other high ranking title. In their worship congregation, nobody leads anything and every item of worship in songs, readings or exhortation is left to the individual worshipper as directed by the Holy Spirit.

In sincerity of purpose, each holder of an office must be properly equipped for the office. Paul depicts the lowest order of the hierarchy as Teacher, meaning Rabbi. It is interesting to note that the office of Rabbi is the highest rank in Judaism. It is the height of knowledge in the Scriptures and Hebrew doctrines and practices. To rise to the office of Teacher in the C & S therefore, demands not only the fulfilment of the Pauline criteria for perfecting the ministry as intimated to Timothy and Titus; but also the ability to teach Scripture and Doctrines of the C & S as well as the ability to articulate the rules and regulations of the church to adherents and inquisitors alike.

Perhaps to indicate that the new order is superior to the old (meaning that the ethos in Christianity is superior to that found in Judaism), it could be said that Paul deliberately places the other four offices above that of the Jewish Rabbi, being the highest in Judaism in their priestly hierarchy! In a similar gesture, he also places the office of Apostle (being an Apostle himself) above that of the Prophet to show that the Prophet needs to be humble and give respect to a higher authority. The above opinions could, however, be taken as more of a socio-political oriented than a genuine spiritual exegetical analysis.

In summary, the hierarchical model of ministry is common to most denominations like the Salvation Army with their military ranks, the Roman Catholics, the Orthodox groups, the Anglicans and other Episcopal denominations. The Cherubim & Seraphim has chosen this kind of ministry in a different way, adopting the Ephesian model. On the other hand, the Egalitarian model is adopted by the Quakers (otherwise known as the Religious Society of Friends), the Baptists and non-Episcopal Methodists. Perhaps Jesus would have opted for Egalitarianism especially considering his resistance to hierarchical wishes of the sons of Zebedee, and his particular teachings on humility.

The Apostles

This office is the highest hierarchy in C & S. Paul as an Apostle himself must have reasons for rating this office as the highest. Apostles are supposed to be good organisers and church planters. They are supposed to possess and master all the attributes of the lower hierarchies. In the C & S, they are vested, by their ordination and anointing, with Apostolic powers and authority to 'fight against principalities, against powers, against the rulers of the darkness of this world, against spiritual wickedness in high places.' The office is supposed to be shrouded with signs and wonders. Holders of this office should be aware of the enormous responsibilities associated with it and work towards perfecting the demands of it. In the C & S tradition, therefore, Apostles pray for people and lay hands on them believing that they are armed with the Apostolic powers for deliverance from adversities and for conferment of God's mercy and favours. This office is supposed to be filled by experienced and spiritually gifted adults in the church. Apostles must always speak with power and authority, guided with wisdom, knowledge and understanding, and inspiration of the Holy Spirit.

Those who aspire and thirst after the office should first read from I Cor 4 for Paul's definition of an apostle. This chapter describes how apostles assume their roles from a position of humility. To serve and not to be served. To be reconciled to the spiritual needs of believers at all levels. To act as custodian of God's truths. To be faithful to the Master, even Jesus Christ our Lord.

The Prophets

The Prophets are supposed to be the mouthpiece of God. The first century church was charismatic and events were Holy Spirit driven. The role of the Prophets was prominent in the early church as believers waited for the direction of the Holy Spirit given through the mouths of Prophets. The Prophets are supposed to cry out against injustice and unholy actions in the church and society. They act as Supervisors (as for Elijah and Elisha) for Visioners and Dreamers, Prophets and Prophetesses-In-Training.

The appointment of Prophets is directed by the Holy Spirit[70]. The other offices in the Ephisian model are dictated by performance of individuals as measured against the criteria given to Timothy and Titus for the offices of a Bishop and a Deacon. Therefore, it is not uncommon to find gifted people who are not anointed because they do not fulfil the criteria and their anointing could damage the respectability and integrity of the ministry. Normally, Prophets develop, after their baptism, by stages:

- Powerful in prayers and given to fasting

- Full of integrity and shrouded in humility, ready to serve than to be served.

- Gifted in undiluted dreams, visions and prophecies

---

70 * Visions and prophecies are recorded during Training Sessions and Prayer Meetings.

These are used to monitor the accuracy of each Dreamer or Visioner as recorded in the Vision Book. From the list of Prophets-In-Training, a few are anointed as Prophets from time to time as the Spirit directs. Where, as it often happens, a church does not follow these steps and arbitrarily ordain without due consideration and the guidance of the Holy Spirit, the result is bound to end up in failure, dysfunctionalism and downfall of the prophet.

- Knowledgeable in Scripture and mastery of the doctrines of the church

- Noted with accuracy consistently in dreams, visions and prophecies.

- Standing as a model of spirituality and blind to vain glories and materialism.

- Abstinence from love of money, alcoholic consumption and lust after flesh and facial beauty.

Prophets are expected to possess greater attributes than those of Seers or Visioners. Elijah and Elisha were able to raise the dead and to perform other miracles. Prophets are expected to be self-disciplined and be given to godliness, fairness and justice. They should be fearless in delivering messages undiluted, as received of the Holy Spirit. They are expected to be more inclined to things spiritual than to things secular. Deliverance from all forms of adversity should be within their ministry and people afflicted with problems physical, mental or spiritual are expected to find solace from their ministry.

Visions and revelations are the hallmarks of prophets. These can appear in different forms to the messenger: The simplest routes to vision include hearing voices and relaying the voices; seeing writings such as on the wall and reading the writings aloud. The more difficult include seeing sceneries and giving interpretations to them. Only the mature and more experienced visioners can give accurate or near accurate interpretations. Sometimes, dialogue is required for a fuller appreciation of the visions. In this case, the visioner has to ask questions on the difficult aspects of the vision and the explanation may come by way of writings or voices. Without engaging in dialogue for this purpose, it can be dangerous to give logical interpretations. Examples of such interpretations are those of Joseph to dreams of the Egyptian Jailer and to that of Pharaoh (Gen. 41); and Daniel's interpretation of the writing on the wall to Belshazzar, the son of Nebuchadnezzar (Dan. 5).

The Evangelists

The Evangelists are supposed to be masters of Scripture and Doctrine of the church.

They should be very apt in preaching and teaching, and principally engaged in outreach evangelism. In Nigeria, such Evangelists would be armed with the Bible and a Hand Bell; going to suitable corners to preach and convert unbelievers to Christ. Some would be engaged in preaching and ringing their hand bells as they travel up and down a street in the early hours of the morning. In this way, people hear the word of God before going out to their daily occupations. Evangelists, therefore, can be seen as 'Street Pastors' as they recruit potential adherents from without the church premises into the fold. Evangelists therefore, are supposed to be impromptu preachers both inside and outside of the church. The Evangelist's role should be seen as a development on that of the Pastor and the Teacher.

In the second part of the 20th century, itinerant evangelists ministered the word of God throughout the world: Billy Graham from America; Morris Cerulo also from America; Garrick Sokari Braid, Moses Orimolade, Joseph Babalola, Josiah Ositelu, Samuel Oshoffa all from Nigeria. These evangelists did not only preach the word of God, they also performed the work of deliverance, healing and miracles wherever they went and through their ministries, multitudes of believers were baptised and referred to any nearby church of various denominations.

The Pastors

These are particularly priestly officers who must be masters of liturgy in the church. They are responsible for the arrangement of Services and appointing officiating officers for each Service. They should be in charge of administration of the Sacraments of Baptism and Holy Communion. Naming Ceremonies, Weddings, visitation to the sick and Funerals. They are supposed to manage the cleanliness of the Prayer House and to welcome and nurture those who attend church Services. The Pastor should oversee the work of the Wardens/Ushers for the maintenance of Law and Order in the Prayer House. Whilst the job of the Evangelist is akin to a Foreign Minister in a government setting, the job of the Pastor is akin to that of the Home Affairs Minister. Because of the nature of their jobs, Pastors are also called Shepherds who are expected to look after the welfare of the sheep or the motivation of the household of the faithful of the Lord. The role of the Pastor should be seen as a logical development of the attributes of a Teacher or Rabbi.

The Teachers

The office of the Teacher is like the training ground for the higher hierarchies in the five-fold ministry. Aspirants for higher offices should acquire more than enough knowledge to teach Scripture and Doctrine at all levels in the church.

Some churches would call a Teacher a Rabbi. A Rabbi is a scholar and expert in the Scriptures in the Judaism. The Jewish community would seek explanation of their spiritual complexities from the Rabbi. Because of this, some followers of Jesus call him Rabbi.

Teachers therefore, in the C & S discourse are responsible for teaching Scripture and Doctrine in the church. They should be adequately equipped to take Bible Study and Sunday School sessions. The office of a Teacher is the beginning of opportunity to demonstrate leadership skills learnt and acquired at the 'Aladura' stage and the opportunity to begin implementation of knowledge learnt. From among the Teachers are appointed Band Officers like President, Secretary, Treasurer and other positions of responsibility. Depending on their level of experiences and skills, they are also suitable candidates for chairing committees.

The older generation in the C & S is mostly knowledgeable in Scripture through studying Religious Knowledge in mainly missionary Schools and Colleges. In this technological and secular era, school children have no preference for Religious Knowledge and most children now leave primary and secondary education without adequate knowledge of Scripture. Hence, for the younger generation, a Bible College or Theological School or Seminary becomes necessary to catch up on Scripture and Doctrine. It should be acknowledged, however, that some children who have missed out from school do manage to catch up a lot through their parents' home lectures and living, and also through Sunday school in their church. Such children are often found on the fast tract to the church ministerial hierarchy.

Ministerial Foundation in the C & S—The Aladuras

The foundation for ministry in the C & S is the ordination of youths and new adherents to the church as 'Aladura.' This is the stage at which the fundamentals of the church are learnt and grasped with all eagerness and enthusiasm. Aladura Brothers and Aladura Sisters must be able to pray fluently for different needs and must be able to memorise and rehearse fluently certain prescribed scriptures, especially from the book of Psalms in addition to the Lord's Prayer, the Seal/Benediction and the Creeds.

The office of Aladura is perhaps the most important in the C & S church. It is the only office held by the founder, Saint Moses Orimolade, who because of his mastery of the attributes of this office, was popularly called and referred to as 'Baba Aladura' by people close to him. The word 'Aladura' means the person who always prays and who is licensed to pray for different needs on behalf of the church. They are otherwise known as 'Prayerists' In some churches, the Aladuras are otherwise called 'Prayer Warriors.' This is because these chosen people are systematically trained and equipped to minister deliverance and healing to those in need.

Such prayer specialists are often requested to visit sick people at home or in the hospital for prayer ministrations, armed by their ordination and assurance that the 'prayer of faith shall save the sick'. The indwelling power of the Holy Spirit works in Aladuras and they should produce results as described in I Cor 12:7-10.

But the manifestation of the Spirit is given to every man to profit withal. For to one is given by the Spirit the word of wisdom; to another the word of knowledge by the same Spirit; to another faith by the same Spirit; to another the gifts of healing by the same Spirit; to another the working of miracles; to another prophecy; to another discerning of spirits; to another diverse kinds of tongues; to another the interpretation of tongues; but all these worketh that one and the selfsame Spirit, dividing to every to every man severally as he will.

The Aladuras, therefore, provide a useful background for the recruitment of able members into the Ephesian 5-hierarchy model. The latter is exclusively in the male domain. From the Aladura foundation, leadership skills are being acquired for further development and implementation at Teacher and/or Lady Leader stages (for female ministries, see below).

Women ministry in the C & S

But the Aladura foundation ministry encompasses both males and females. What has not been mentioned so far is the ministry of women in the C & S. Throughout the growth of the church, different ordination grades have been proposed to suit talented women in the church. It is arguable that if females can perform brilliantly as Aladuras, why are they not eligible for ordination into the Ephesian 5-hierarchy? The answer relates to the exclusion by Paul the Apostle, demanding that women should be silent in church (ICor 14:34). It is to be recognised that Paul formulated most of the doctrines of the church. But in C & S like most other churches, women always form the majority in membership. The proportion of members blessed with spiritual gifts is higher within the women fold than in men fold. In contrast to Paul's doctrine on women ministry, the C & S church has recognised the need to channel female gifts in the most sensible way that does not compromise the masculinity and male domain of the Ephesian 5-hierarchy. This is in order to maximise utilisation of all gifts in the church for a greater edification of the membership. Beyond the office of Aladura, which could be called homemade and peculiar to the C & S, there has been found adequate and admirable female leadership roles in both the Old and New Testaments.

Mothers-In-Israel

Deborah as a judge, was the first Mother-In-Israel (Judges 4 & 5). This is the highest ordination given to mature and experienced women in the church. Holders of this high office should be able to command the respect of all women. In the absence of men elders in an assembly, they take control of the proceedings and pronounce absolution and seal all prayers. This office is the equivalence of the office of Apostles for men. In most small to medium congregations, there is usually one such Mother-In-Israel who could also be the Church Mother. In larger congregations, there may be several Mothers-In-Israel, out of which the most senior and experienced is chosen to be the Church Mother.

Prophetesses

There are women leaders holding the office of Prophetess in the Old Testament: Mirian, the sister of Moses and Aaron; Deborah who was a judge in Israel; Anna, the daughter of Phanuel of the tribe of Aser, who was given to fasting and prayers in the temple as a widow for eighty-four years. Anna, like Simeon, gave thanks to God at the blessing of Jesus at the temple. After Anna, there is no mention of any prophetess in the New Testament. The Prophetess is taken as the equivalent of the Prophet in the C & S church. They carry similar staff and perform similar duties in the church.

Prophets and Prophetesses should not have any allegiance to any Band in the church. Once anointed, they become the servants of the whole church and must be prepared to minister to all equitably. This is in order to prevent any temptation to unhealthy rivalry between prophets within themselves and groups or bands in the church. The prophets where they are many, could be grouped into a band such as Aaron or Daniel Band.

Lady Leaders

The office of Lady Leader is the offshoot of that of the Mother-In-Israel as the former is not particularly mentioned in the Bible. A Lady Leader must have similar attributes as that of a Teacher. An extension of this office is created as Senior Lady Leaders to correspond to the office of the Pastor and the Evangelist. Lady Leaders and Senior Lady Leaders should be mature elders capable of leading a band in the church. From among them are appointed Presidents and Officers of Bands. They should be able to motivate their members in the Band and be self-disciplined. They are expected to be role models laying good examples and showing love and godliness.

The following table can be taken as drawing the equivalence of male and female ordination grades across the churches. Any other grades are not biblical and are mere decorations of the 5-hierarchy. As for C & S construction for females, the offices of Mother-In-Israel and Prophetess are biblical and the others are extensions of female leadership positions modelled on the fundamental attributes of a Mother-In-Israel.

The Ephesian 5-hierarchy male model	Constructed C & S Female Equivalent
Apostle	Mother-In-Israel
Prophet	Prophetess
Evangelist	Senior Lady Leader
Pastor	Senior Lady Leader
Teacher	Lady Leader

Mode of Ministry

Holders of these offices are ministers of the Word who should be assigned particular portfolios such as Band Presidents, Secretaries, Treasurers, Deacons*, Committee Chair Persons etc. Ordination should therefore, be carried out to fill such portfolios.

When people are ordained without holding any assigned positions in the church, they can best be described as 'ministers without portfolio' Apparently for political and sentimental reasons, such ordinations are more common in many of our churches today. It can be argued that ordinations without assigned portfolios have more often bred rivalries and for positions and power in the church.

Borne out of unhealthy competition for status within members and between churches a more recent (and rather ridiculous) development is the undesirable addition to the biblical 5-hierarchy Model, with the introduction of unnecessary adjectives like: Senior, Most Senior, Special, Most Special, Superintendent, Senior Superintendent, General Superintendent, Superior this, Superior that etc. Jesus would be grieved at the introduction of these adjectives into His ministry, should He return today. Despite pressure from some of His followers like the sons of Zebedee, He did not call Peter, James and John anything more than simply, Apostles. Jesus was more egalitarian than hierarchical in His approach to ministry. His teaching was more focused on humility than the vanity of pride, arrogance and futility. He did not differentiate Himself from his disciples even in dress codes. No wonder Judas Iscariot had to identify him by kissing before the High Priests could arrest him.

Deacons *

Unlike the Ephesian 5-Hierarchy model, Deacons are not strictly into priestly ordination category, but more into secular and administrative; despite the same prerequisite criteria for both. Priestly ordination grades are essentially spiritual and priestly but Deacons occupy more secular offices like Church Secretaries, Wardens, Ushers, Treasurers, Gate Keepers, Security Officers, Maintenance Officers, Law and Order Officers etc. According to Acts 6:1-4, the first seven Deacons were appointed by the people themselves to relieve the Apostles of routine administration so that the latter could concentrate on spiritual and more strategic matters. For these reasons, people should not be ordained into, but be appointed to the office of Deacons, upon vacancies arising in any particular calling. It should be remembered that the Apostles received divine calling by Jesus personally; but the Deacons were appointed by the people upon demand for supplementary ministry. However, transfers from one category into the other upon necessity cannot be ruled out as the criteria for recruitment into both are the same.

The interpretation given to the office of a Deacon in C & S is nearest to the Presbyterian Church model, where the Deacon is a layman attending to secular affairs of the congregation; and in other Non-conformist Churches, where the Deacon is one of a body elected to advise and assist pastors to administer charities and attend to secular matters.

CHAPTER 9

THE CHERUBIM & SERAPHIM LITURGY

The C & S Epistemology is fondly shrouded with prayer more than anything else in our liturgy. Some members and Elders have even proudly claimed that 'prayer is our business'. This claim is directed to urge members to learn to focus on prayer for solution to most needs; and to cultivate the belief in wholesomeness in religion. Most Christians happen to live ambivalent lives by worshipping God in words, and not in deed. Jesus describes such people as similar to Isaiah's prophecy:

This people honoureth me with their lips, but their heart is far from me (Mark 7:6)

As a result, such people like to be seen as relying whole heartedly on God for solution to everything, but in practice, they seek other gods in the time of crisis. But God is capable of providing all solutions. Before God all things are possible. To enjoy this grace requires believers to live according to God's precepts; so that a perfect union is formed with the believer living in Jesus, who lives in God the Father, who through the Holy Spirit makes everything possible. Jesus pleaded:

Abide in me, and I in you. As the branch cannot bear fruit of itself, except it abide in the vine, no more can ye, except ye abide in me. I am the vine, ye are the branches: he that abideth in me, and I in him, the same bringeth forth much fruit; for without me ye can do nothing (John 15: 4-5)

Cherubim & Seraphim Epistemology

This is the basis on which believers can achieve success without seeking other gods or other means of achieving their goals. This is the only way that God will make possible what the world thinks is not possible. With Jesus, all things are possible. Without Jesus, nothing can be possible. This is a matter of choice for the wise.

Both divine Service and weekday Prayer Meeting or Shiloh Service are packed with prayers of one sort or the other. In both instances, more time is spent on prayers than any other item. Even choice songs or hymns are particularly in tune with the type of Service or prayer on hand. Most of the hymns and songs are prayers themselves. Let us go through a typical liturgy for a divine Service as adopted by the Cherubim & Seraphim Council of Churches in 1976 in Nigeria:

1. Ante Processional Prayer
2. Processional Hymn
3. Introit
4. Opening Hymn
5. Opening Prayers: Reading of 3 Psalms followed by
   i. Prayers for Confession of sins (after short adoration phrases)
   ii. Sanctification,
   iii. Descent of the Holy Spirit,
   iv. The Lord's Prayer &
   v. The Seal
6. Thanksgiving Hymn (1 or 3) followed by 3 choruses in Praise & Worship

The Cherubim & Seraphim Liturgy

7. Thanksgiving Prayer & Seal
8. First Lesson Reading from the Old Testament followed by a hymn or Canticle/Gloria
9. Second Lesson Reading from the New Testament followed by a hymn or Canticle/Gloria
10. The Creed (usually Apostles' Creed or Nicene Creed when there is Holy Communion)
11. Prayers of Intercession (usually called 3 Peoples' Prayers)
12. Visions and Revelations followed by Prayers for the revelations
13. Announcements
14. Hymn Before Sermon
15. Sermon
16. Testimonies and Thanksgivings
17. Sundry Activities
18. Closing Hymn
19. Closing Prayers
20. Vesper
21. Silent Prayers
22. Benediction
23. Recessional Hymn
24. Post Recessional Prayer and Dismissal

Hymnology

Many hymns are sung during a divine Service. The chosen hymn or song must essentially resonate with the nature of the item in the programme of the Service.

There is usually a good choice from a list of hymns and the most relevant are chosen to augment a particular item in a programme. Many of the hymns are conventional songs that are common to most denominations. Most of the hymns are songs composed by indigenous members, especially by prophets who sang the hymns first during their period of being in trance. Such songs are recorded and later adopted as hymns to be used in worship. Such songs are not inter-denominational except where copied or adapted by other denominations. It can always be a pride to see other older or newer denominations who can discern spiritual value in Cherubim & Seraphim songs; and who choose to copy or adapt them to enrich their own spirituality and worship.

Processional Hymns (2)

The hymns chosen are usually introductory such as 'Onward Christian Soldiers marching as to war' or 'Who are these like stars appearing'. They are meant to summon worshippers to be on alert and ready to worship.

Introit (3) & Vesper (20)

Introit and Vesper are usually short and meant to introduce or conclude a Service. They could be specially composed short songs or one verse of a hymn that fulfils the purpose of introduction or conclusion.

Opening Hymn (4)

Selection of the Opening Hymn is usually from a list of hymns containing adoration and invocation of the Holy Spirit like 'Holy, holy, holy, Lord God Almighty' or 'King of Saints to whom the numbers of the starry host is known'.

Opening Prayers (5)

The opening prayer follows a particular systematic order. The order is meant to approach worship with humility by confessing individual sins and asking for forgiveness. The opening prayer is made richer if preceded by short phrases of adoration to acknowledge the awesomeness and the mightiness of God. A plea for sanctification follows, and the third component is invocation of the Holy Spirit to take control and champion the programme of worship Service from the beginning to the end.

Sometimes, the third component is mistakenly diverted to invocation of the 'Heavenly Hosts'. The latter are angelic beings and should not be worshipped or called upon in any worship Service. The angels receive orders only from the Almighty God and not from any man. Therefore, the inclusion of Holy Michael, Holy Gabriel, Holy Raphael and Holy Euriel in any opening prayer or any other prayer for that matter should not be encouraged as such habit is grossly erroneous.

The three components are followed by the Lord's Prayer and the Seal. The importance of the Seal is discussed under a separate heading. It is necessary here to stress the importance of the Opening Prayer. It is not just a matter of formality but a serious time to express soberness and humility before the awesome God;

as He is always ready to extend His mercy to those who turn unto Him with a penitent heart:

If my people, which are called by my name, shall humble themselves, and pray, and seek my face, and turn from their wicked ways; then will I hear from heaven, and will forgive their sin, and will heal their land. (2 Chr. 7:14)

It is after this rite of absolution that the rest of the worship Service can proceed smoothly and be followed with rejoicing, thanksgiving, sharing of the Word and petitions or intercession prayers for more mercies from the Lord. It is therefore vital for every worshipper to be part of the Opening Prayer for the fullness of blessings.

Thanksgiving Hymn (6) & Thanksgiving Prayer(7)

Thanksgiving occupies a most important aspect of Cherubim & Seraphim worship. It is very often mentioned that our thanks in prayer should be greater than our requests. Thanksgiving in songs and prayers illuminates the believer's appreciation and gratefulness to God for His mercies which are unmerited by man. Therefore, whether sung or spoken, thanksgiving should highlight the magnanimity of God's love and kindness at all times. That is the reason why very often, many hymns and songs of praise are offered to God, despite the fact that they can be time consuming.

The Cherubim & Seraphim Church of Zion (Ilaje/Igbonla) worship is a typical brand of African worship in which God's faithfulness is always highlighted in songs and dancing. It is in Yoruba dominated congregations often accompanies by trumpets, African drums in the musical section and tambourines, marakas 'shekere[71]' in the congregation. One needs to listen to the chanting of Mary's song of praise to the Almighty God after the annunciation of her immaculate conception by angel Gabriel; and upon her visit to her cousin, Elizabeth (John the Baptist's mother) who testified to the blessedness of Mary as 'the mother of my Lord' (Lk1:43). Mary's song (The Magnificat) is popularly sung in the liturgies of Roman Catholic, Orthodox and Anglican churches; as well as in Cherubim & Seraphim churches, as one of the Canticles (Lk 1:46-55) followed by the Gloria after the reading of a Scripture.

Lesson Readings (8) & (9)

Whenever convenient, the First Lesson from the Old Testament is usually read by a female; whilst the Second, from the New Testament is read by a male. This rule does not apply when the congregation is predominantly female or male. It is one aspect of the C & S Epistemology in which participation in officiating is inclusive irrespective of sex or age. All are given the opportunity for self development; so that nobody will be hearer only, but doers of the Word.

Intercession Prayers (Otherwise known as Three Peoples' Prayer) (11)

These prayers are sectioned into three parts; taken by three Elders: male, female and male in that order. The session is loaded with various prayer requests in no particular order but covering personal and corporate needs such as Mercy, Deliverance, Protection,

---

[71] A calabash with a mesh of beads on the outside, shaken to the beat of the music.

Healing, Spiritual Powers, Steadfastness, Provision, Spiritual Directions for Heads of States and Head of Churches. These needs and any others are sectioned into three and undertaken by three Elders as above outlined. A Seal is applied after the three prayers by an authorised Elder for efficacy.

Visions and Revelations (12)

Officially, visions and revelations (if any) are delivered by authorised visioners immediately after the Intercession Prayers. The order of delivery is usually from bottom to top in the church hierarchy; females followed by males. Occasionally, visions may be given at any other times during the Service by authorised Visioners as the Spirit directs; but with approval necessarily by the church Leader. If approval is denied, then the visioner will be required to deliver privately to a recorder who will later refer the visions to the Leader to deal with at their discretion.

At the end of delivery, all visions are covered with Congregational Prayers or a prayer by an authorised Elder for speedy delivery of all positives; and eradication of the negative aspects of the visions. It is then sealed by an authorised Elder.

The Sermon (15)

This can be preached from the pulpit in ordinary worship Service or from the floor of the Prayer House in a Revival Service. Revival Sermons are usually more elaborate and longer than usual Sermons. The Sermon is usually preached directly from the pulpit; whilst the Revival can be both from the pulpit and/or from the floor of the Prayer House. The nature of the Sermon can vary depending on the extent of participation by the congregation. Sometimes, the Preacher can be interrupted by a song or Bible quotation by some members. It is up to the Preacher to accept or to decline such interruptions. But when it happens, such interruptions are usually seen not as a distraction; but as enrichment to the theme of the sermon whenever they are relevant. It also provides motivation for participating members as signs of growth in their potential for leadership.

Testimonies & Thanksgiving (16)

This section in the liturgy is a time for members to publicly narrate their success stories of how the power of prayer and the work of the Holy Spirit have impacted their lives and experiences. This is done in order following the hierarchy bottom to top on the female side, before the same on the male side. Time management is crucial at this time for the conductor depending on how many members wish to give open testimonies. Some testimonies and thanksgiving can alternatively be 'silent' when the member does not come out to speak, but writes their testimonies in outline for the conductor to read publicly to the hearing of the congregation.

Other members with testimonies simply remain anonymous; they neither speak openly nor write out their testimonies for announcement, but only make their donations during collections for Testimonies and Thanksgivings, after thanking God in their hearts. All formats are prayed for and believed to be equally acceptable to God.

Sundry Activities (17)

At the discretion of the Leader of the church, this is the space for all sorts of activities such as Sprinkling and Anointing, Naming

Ceremonies, Consecration of water, Special Presentations such as Biblical Drama, Army of Salvation parade, Report of any special assignments that call for congregational hearing. Any other activity can always be loaded under this heading. All other items on the Programme of worship Service are self explanatory and require little or no elaboration.

Christening of Babies

In the C & S Epistemology, babies are Christened and/or blessed before the congregation on or after they become eight days old, if male; or forty days old if female. If the baby is not ready for blessing at these ages, then the blessing can take place before the age of twelve years, after which full baptism by immersion becomes possible. These are modifications of the Leviticus Laws as outlined in Chapter 12. The C & S Christening is based on the presentation of Jesus in the Temple at eight days old when he was blessed by Simeon (Lk 2:25) and witnessed by Anna the prophetess (Lk 2:36).

Jesus was not baptised until he was thirty years old. He was baptised in the River Jordan by immersion as all others by his cousin, John the Baptist. The C & S also believe in Believers' baptism by immersion at the minimum age of twelve. It is our belief that twelve is the minimum age of reasoning for the average child. At that age, Jesus was found:

In the temple, sitting in the midst of the doctors, both hearing them, and asking them questions. And all that heard him were astonished at his understanding and answers (Lk. 2:46-47)

When critics query the necessity of waiting to baptise a child (especially in case the child dies before the age of twelve), the simple answer we give is that our choice of the Biblical blessing of the child is based on the belief that the blessing is as good for salvation as Believers' baptism for adults; and also for formal admission into the family of God prior to believers' baptism. The latter is repentance oriented and it is crucial to the pledge to change from sin into the righteousness of God. The former on the other hand, is based on the premise of dedication to God before growing and capable of indulging in sinfulness.

The Christening of children can be performed at the parents' home or in the Prayer House. Three symbolic elements are used in the process: water, salt and honey. seven white candles are also lit. The water represents prayer for the gift of life; the salt represents prayer for adding value to the quality of life; and the honey represents prayer for wisdom, as the Bible describes honey as the food of prophets. The seven candles represent prayer for divine presence in the life of the child, as the figure seven represents completeness or perfection. God created the world in six days and rested on the seventh. His creation was complete and after inspection, it was found satisfactory. The use of the three symbolic elements may be rightly described as a matter of African inculturation. But it is definitely not paganist but grounded in the Scriptures as directed by the Holy Spirit.

The Officiating Minister carries the baby in his hands and touching each of the elements with a finger, he places a microscopic amount in the lips of the baby, pronouncing the given names audibly in the name of the Father, and of the Son, and of the Holy Spirit each time. After the pronouncement of the names, seven Elders are invited to surround the baby, still in the hand of the

Minister; and to pray variously for protection, good health, long life, provision, wisdom, knowledge and understanding amongst other blessings. The naming ceremony is then concluded with a Seal over the prayers by the Presiding Minister.

Believers' Baptism

There are different kinds of baptism across Christian denominations. Some perform baptism by sprinkling water on the candidate and others do it by total immersion. Some baptise all ages either by sprinkling or by immersion. Of those who baptise by immersion, some dip the candidate once and others, thrice. The directive in the Gospel of Matthew commands baptism to be done:

in the name of the Father, and of the Son, and of the Holy Ghost. (Matt. 28:19)

While some denominations follow this formula but dip the candidate in the water once, the C & S and some other denominations dip the candidate into the water thrice. One dip in the name of the Father; another dip in the name of the Son; and a third dip in the name of the Holy Spirit. After that, the sign of the cross is marked on the forehead of the candidate to conclude the rite.

The C & S does not condemn the alternative model (the Unitarian model) where the candidate is dipped into the water only once:

In the name of Jesus Christ (Acts 2:38)

as practised by the Apostles. This kind of baptism by immersion is known as 'Jesus only' or 'Unitarian' as adherents of the model assert that baptism in the name of 'Jesus only' is sufficient as he (Jesus) is the Father as well as the Holy Spirit. The Unitarians believe that the earthly name of God is Jesus, who came to us in the flesh, and also came back as the Holy Spirit after his ascension to heaven.

CHAPTER 10
UNIQUENESS OF C & S EPISTEMOLOGY

The Cherubim & Seraphim Church is one of the churches that many observers find difficult to understand in terms of classification and typology. Many people have asked whether the church is Pentecostal, Charismatic, Roman Catholic, Anglican or even whether it is a Christian church at all! This is because several things are done differently as compared with what obtains in other denominations. What cannot be disputed is the fact that any aspect of the doctrine and practice of the church is firmly grounded in Scripture. The following are some of the peculiar attributes of the church:

Hygiene codes

For a start, some tend to think that the C & S is too close to Islam because of similarities in our hygiene codes; not wearing shoes in worship, women and men separately seated in the Prayer House and particularly banning of anything considered as unclean, blemish and/or abomination such as dead bodies and blood. Hence, the restraint of females in their menstrual periods from attending Divine Services and Prayer Meetings. These hygiene codes were ordered by the Founder, Moses Orimolade, and not necessarily following Leviticus narratives. There are valid spiritual imperatives that prompted the impositions.

There must be some important reasons why God commanded Moses to remove his shoes (Ex. 3:5); and why the captain of the

Lord's host commanded Joshua to do similarly because in both cases, holiness was called for. God will not communicate with man in an unclean and unholy environment because light and darkness cannot mix. Any unhealthy and dirty environment is never conducive to free operation of the Holy Spirit. That is why Paul asked:

What fellowship hath righteousness with unrighteousness? And what communion hath light with darkness? (2 Cor.6:14)

Even though Moses and Joshua in their obedience to the commands could not claim perfect cleanliness in their encounters with the Divine, yet the wearing of their shoes could certainly complicate their uncleanliness and so make divine communication difficult if not impossible. It is quite recognised that Jesus condemned outward cleanliness as hypocrisy:

Woe unto you, scribes and Pharisees, hypocrites! for you are like whited sepulchres, which indeed appear beautiful outward, but are within full of dead men's bones, and of all uncleanness. (Matt. 23:27)

It also needs to be recognised that Jesus meant outward cleanness without inward cleanness accompanying. Both inward and outward must necessarily go together to reach perfection or at least near perfection. All efforts must therefore be made to keep the Prayer House clean as much as possible; and worshippers also, should observe the hygiene code as much as possible, both in body and in spirit. Moses and Joshua were commanded and they obeyed. The results of their missions were successful. The command of our Leader, Moses Orimolade is equally valid. Give it a chance and obey the command; and like for Moses and Joshua, the result must be well.

Colour codes

White signifies purity.

As a white garment church, Prayer Gowns are basically in white colour. Head covers in either hats or veils are also in white. When there is a call for Unity Prayers, only white colour is encouraged for Prayer Gowns, Girdles and Head covers.

Blue signifies love.

Blue Girdles are usually worn on white Prayer Gowns on Sundays by any member irrespective of hierarchy. Where there is any Band such as Love Divine, their favourite colour is blue. New members who are not yet ordained usually wear either white or blue Girdles.

Yellow represents the glowing fire of the Holy Spirit.

Members who have been ordained into any hierarchy may wear Yellow Girdles especially for Sunday worship.

Purple signifies royalty.

Members in the highest hierarchy are permitted to wear Purple Girdles or Prayer Gowns for worship as representing prospective Princes or Princesses of the Kingdom.

Red represents blood

It represents the shedding of the blood of Christ on the hill of Calvary. Hence, red is worn either in Prayer Gowns, Girdles or both on Good Fridays and on Saint Michael's Day Services.

Saint Michael Day is formally celebrated by C & S to honour her Patron Saint annually on 29th September. Michael was the humble angel empowered by the sevenfold powers of the Almighty God to confront and overthrow Lucifer when there was war in heaven according to the book of Revelation chapter 12.

Red Girdles are usually worn on Weekday or Shiloh Prayers as they are usually Prayers of Intercession especially for Deliverance and Healing.

Participative Worship

The C & S worship is more participative than can be seen in any other church. It is like being the disciples of James who pleaded:

But be ye doers of the word, and not hearers only, deceiving your own selves. For if any be a hearer of the word, and not a doer, he is like unto a man beholding his natural face in a glass; for the beholdeth himself, and goeth his way, and straightway forgetteth what manner of man he was (James 1:22-24).

For this reason, self development is encouraged across gender and generational divides: men and women; young and old; members and guests, clergy and laity. For the same reason, it is always difficult for any visitor to spot who is the Leader, Pastor or Minister in Charge during our worship in all congregations; as several members are officiating in one capacity or the other. It is not all members that can adequately perform every function in the church liturgy. Certain members are quite good in one function or the other. Such members are in the majority. But a few other members are multi-talented. Some start from being single talented and remain so but grow in intensity. Others aspire to become multi-talented and so develop step by step. Everyone who shows aptitude for self-development at whatever level is given a chance to come out of passivity and into proactive and positivity. That way, potential leaders can be identified and lined up for future leadership succession plan.

The Amen factor

Members are always encouraged to shout Amen, not only at the end of prayers, but also during a prayer intermittently whenever a sentence calls for approval of the hearers. This habit fosters concentration of the congregation in the prayer being said; and promotes efficacy of prayer. At the end of each prayer, a loud Amen is said three times to lay emphasis on the whole prayer request. An observer asked whether this habit of saying Amen thrice makes the C & S more Trinitarian than other Christians. It is not the 'Amen' only that is said thrice in our worship. The shouts of Hallelujah, Hossanah and Iye are also shouted thrice most times.

An observer once remarked that in Pentecostal Churches in particular, the shout of 'Hallelujah' and 'Praise the Lord' are said sporadically but that in C & S the shouts are regularised and said sometimes, once, thrice, seven times, twenty one times or even forty two times. This number of times has spiritual meaning to them.

- One shout represents the unity of the trinity (three in one);
- Three shouts represent the revelation of God in three forms (one in three)
- Seven shouts represent the seven fold powers of the Almighty God[72]

---

[72] Google Source. The 7 Spirits of God are mentioned 4 times in the Book of Isaiah and in the Book of Revelation. Of particular relevance in this context is Rev.4:5 & 5:6.

- Twenty One and forty two represent multiples of the seven.

This culture of counting numbers also features in the way we light candles during divine worship and in prayer meetings. The lighting of candles also accounts for differences between C & S and the Pentecostals; and even many in the AIC. The use of candles is not just to dispel nights's gloom but also to represent Christ, the uncreated and Eternal Light[73]. Those that are not conversant with the use tend to equate it to satanic worship! There are certainly aspects of these in Anglo-Catholic worship but very scarce in other Christian denominations. Number counting and the use of candles are very common in Judaism and certainly in the Apocalypse Scripture.

It cannot therefore be said that C & S is necessarily pro-Old Testament. The church believes and lives in the New Testament but does not discard the Old. It should be recognised that Jesus himself was never a Christian. He was born into Judaism. He lived and died in the religion. He warned that he had not come to dissolve but to fulfil the Law. The New Testament, therefore, is the fulfilment of the Old, not the dissolution of it.

Think not that I am come to destroy the law, or the prophets; I am not come to destroy, but to fulfil. For verily I say unto you, till heaven and earth pass, one jot or one tittle shall in no wise pass from the law; till all be fulfilled. Whosoever therefore shall break one of these least commandments, and shall teach men so, he shall be called the least in the kingdom of heaven: but whosoever shall do and teach them, the same shall be called great in the kingdom of heaven. (Matt. 5:17-19)

---

73 Google source.

His focus was limited to cleansing and renewing the misconceptions in Judaism. A Bible scholar once described the Old Testament as Scripture proper; and the New Testament as the Biography of Jesus and Counselling of his followers. This assessment of the Scripture is quite compatible with the C & S Epistemology.

The Seal and sealing of prayers.

Another unique practice in C&S church is the sealing of prayers. Immediately after an Elder finishes a prescribed prayer, a seal becomes necessary to conclude the prayer. The seal is a short confirmation of the main prayer by an appointed Elder. The prerogative usually lies with the Leader who is looked up to as charged with power and authority for efficacy. The latter is the key and finality to all prayers. Sometimes the sealing can be delegated to another Elder who must essentially be holder of a high office in the church hierarchy; or that he is a young Leader of Service who has been in prayer and fasting prior to leading the Service.

The whole emphasis on sealing is derived from divine anointing bestowed on special people like Aaron and his children with divine assignment to minister in the office of priesthood to the household of Israel; or on old people or father of the house who has given up worldliness and particularly who has covenanted to

have clean hands and a pure heart; who hath not lifted up his soul unto vanity, nor sworn deceitfully. He shall receive the blessing from the Lord, and righteousness from the God of his salvation (Ps. 24:4/5).

Such people in the Bible are Abraham, Isaac and Jacob. A glaring example is the blessing of Jacob and Esau by their father Isaac. Once the latter pronounced the bigger blessing on Jacob (although

Uniqueness of C & S Epistemology

mistakenly) it could not be withdrawn or corrected when Esau (who had right to the bigger blessing) arrived. What is very important is that the blessing was divinely charged with power and authority which could neither be changed nor withdrawn.

So shall my word be that goeth forth out of my mouth, it shall not return unto me void, but it shall accomplish that which I please, and it shall prosper in the thing whereto I sent it (Isaiah 55:11)

Similarly, Jacob also blessed his twelve children differently according to his perception of their individual characters; and each blessing is today reflected in the lives of the twelve tribes of Israel. Although each tribe derives from the same father, the pronouncement of blessing on them are differently weighted and disproportional. It is similar to a dying father making his will for his surviving children or family. This is the origin of the Seal in C & S Epistemology. It is different to the Benediction which is commonly said by all denominations and usually pronounced at the very end of a Worship Service or Prayer Meeting, by the presiding clergy or his appointee. The Seal in Yoruba cosmology is known as 'Ase'. It is a form of spiritual power, or 'holy magic' described as:

The unseen principle of efficacy that emanates from God and articulates his creation through a web of energy[74]

It is interesting to note that

The impact of spiritual power in orthodox christian discourse, as communicated through its central text, is heavily reduced. The vital principle of 'ase' (seal) sits awkwardly in mainstream Christianity, which

---

[74] Harris, Hermione, *Yoruba in Diaspora, an African Church in London*, pelgrave macmillan 2006 p55.

emphasises morality more than miracles. The ineffability of spiritual energy is exchanged for the prosaic concept of divine omnipotence, confirming God's majesty, not his magic[75]

A seal, though shorter than the main prayer is rather more weighty than the main prayer itself; because it is pronounced by an anointed minister, whether young or old.

It is therefore a prerequisite for efficacy in any prayer ministration in the C & S Epistemology. The seal is one of the contributing factors to prayer efficacy in the church, and if taken out, and efficacy is deflated, then the church would follow the path of most Christian denominations in shedding thaumaturgy and ethereal gifts.

The seal is pronounced by an Elder

with an innate metaphysical power who by virtue of this power maintains complete and awesome control over spiritual realms and, by extension, over social ones ... performative power, the power of accomplishment, the power to get things done, to make things happen[76]

The seal (ase) is, therefore, what turns ordinary into extraordinary. It is the unseen performative force that delivers miracles. It turns the natural into super-natural. It is the whole essence of bringing heavenly grace down to earth. The concept of sealing prayers is one of the offerings of Cherubim & Seraphim to the ecumenical community for the enhancement of spirituality; and it is worth emulating for those who do thirst for practical (as opposed to

---

75 Ibid, p60.'

76 Ibid p58

theoretical) Christianity; those who appreciate substance in (as opposed to rhetorical) worshipping.

Eschatology Scenarios

In most medium and large congregations in the C & S, youth activities include organising of uniformed 'Army of Salvation' (in some C & S churches such as 'Movement' similar set up is called 'The Brigade' in Blue uniforms) which is different to 'The Salvation Army' as a denomination and Registered Charity; but with similarity in uniform, character and ranking. The vision of the latter is to seek the fullness of life for all with Jesus; and their mission is:

- To share the Good News;
- To serve others without discrimination;
- To nurture disciples of Jesus;
- To care for creation and
- To seek justice and reconciliation.

On the other hand, the mission of Cherubim & Seraphim 'Army of Salvation' is principally, inter alia, to:

- serve a congregation to maintain law and order;
- minister to the needs of members and Elders;
- oversee the security of members and their properties;
- provide training in scripture and doctrine of the church;
- teach the youths in church ethics and discipline;

- induct youths against anti-social tendencies;

- mentor the Soldiers on proactive initiatives and community cohesion.

Membership of the Army of Salvation is open to males and females of all ages. The ranks are highly hierarchical from Corporals to Colonels, Brigadiers, Generals, Field Marshals and other ranks according to age, length of membership and experience. Together, they are known and called 'Soldiers' One of the highlights of the Army is the display of military-style parades and marching during special occasions as time permits. Commands are issued by Senior Officers and orders are carried out by the junior ranks. Sometimes, it is interesting to see especially infant members when they get mixed up when the orders are issued so rapidly, getting the infants confused as to where to turn, right, left and about-turns!

The Soldiers also learn and present systematic dances to the rhythm of most hymns and choruses during liturgical songs. Such presentations are aimed at motivating worshippers and to boost the morale of the members. Rather than be seen as a distraction to the liturgy, they can actually be valued as motivating factors to divine worship, and reducing any boredom arising from a prolonged Service. The activities of the Soldiers represent a foretaste of heavenly worship and a reminder that we can worship God on earth, as it is in heaven. They also prepare members for the hitherto elusive Rapture, when the Lord will reign on earth indefinitely.

The Prophetic Ministry.

The Cherubim & Seraphim church encourages training and development of this vital ministry for the edification of her membership.

Occasionally during the Divine Worship, and particularly after the Intercession Prayers, time is given for accredited

Visioners to articulate their visions and revelations to the congregation. This aspect of liturgy is not very common in other denominations. Sometimes visioners deliver their messages in the language everyone can understand. Sometimes they speak in tongues. The experienced visioners who speak in tongues sometimes interpret their own tongues; whilst others require interpretation by others gifted for the purpose. When any visioner speaks in tongues and no interpretation is available, such visioners are encouraged to stop in order to minimise disruption in the Service. Such control helps to facilitate the smooth running of the Service.

The quality of vision delivery is very crucial to the motivation of the congregation at all times. Any substandard delivery is usually referred to the attention of a Senior Prophet or Supervising Prophet to apply any or necessary corrective measure to improve on the standard. Edification is the watchword of vision delivery and any meaningless or impresario syndromes are discouraged.

Ringing of Bells

Apart from ringing Bells to complement musical instruments during singing, Bells are rung thrice at the beginning of a Service especially after singing the Introit. It is also rung thrice after the Benediction. The ringing after the Introit signifies the summoning of the heavenly hosts to assemble with the worshippers; whilst the ringing after the Benediction signifies the dismissal of the same in thanksgiving. It is the C & S alternative to the Tower Bells rung prior to the commencement of Divine Services as practised by Orthodox and Mission Churches. Their Bells are rung from their church towers, whilst ours are rung from the Altar Tables. Both methods signal the same message of summoning heavenly and earthly worshippers to assemble before God.

Ringing the Bells when singing is so central to the upliftment of members that the congregation sometimes sing an appropriate chorus that shows the level of determination to bring heavenly worship to the earth; singing words of expectation like:

I'm going to ring those heavenly Bells, when I get there,
I'm going to ring those heavenly Bells, when I get there;
My sorrows will be over, my heavenly joy comes over;
I'm going to ring those heavenly Bells, when I get there.

The words of the song serve to consolidate the expectation of the Rapture and the belief that our sufferings in this world will be compensated with rich rewards 'when I get there'. This perspective shows the level and depth of the Eschatological enthusiasm that is pertinent in the thinking of most members.

Regularities and Irregularities

It cannot be argued that the C & S is noted for shouting praises to God a number of times: once, thrice, seven and even more times. The three number of shouts particularly is ascribed to the Father, Son and Holy Spirit (three in one, and one in three). It cannot also be argued that all factions of the C & S believe in applying the three pattern formula to Hallelujah, Hosanna and Iye (Salvation). In shouting the first two, all hands are raised pointing up (admittedly to God in heaven). During the third shout of Iye, all hands are lowered to different directions; some to touch the head, and some to touch the chest (where the heart is).

Uniqueness of C & S Epistemology

In these processes, there are two main disparities. First is the disparity between touching of the 'head' by some; and of the 'chest' by others is a misconception in shouting of Iye (Salvation). The simple reason is that the head holds the brain, whilst the chest holds the heart. The Hebrew catechism states that

Thou shalt love the Lord thy God with all thine heart; and with all thy soul, and with all thy might. (Deut. 6:5)

The scripture does not say 'with all thy head'; nor does it say 'with all thy brain'; but 'with all thine heart'. Therefore, the placing of the hands while shouting Iye, should rightly be on the chest, where the heart is. This reference should be enough to settle disparities on where to place the hands in shouting 'Iye'.

Secondly, 'Iye' is basically not a shout of praise to God. It is more of a petition to God for human salvation. If, as it is assumed, the shoutings are ascribed to honour God, and especially to honour the Trinity, it should not have been included in the three shoutings at all, because 'praise and adoration' to God should not be mixed with 'petition' which belongs to prayers of intercession for man. Mixing 'Iye' with 'Hallelujah and Hosanna' looks like sharing the glory of God with man. God has specifically objected to sharing His glory with anyone and said:

I am the Lord; that is my name, and my glory will I not give to another, neither my praise to graven images. (Isaiah 43:8)

If, therefore, the inclusion of 'Iye' amounts to violating God's objection in this matter, a substitute should be found to complete the three shouts of praise to the Trinity. A choice could be made from other words like, honour, glory, power, might, majesty, dominion and such other words of praise to appreciate the mightiness of God. This should be one of the thoughts of delegates to the Annual General Conference of the church; and which should trigger dialogue amongst members who believe and practise the shoutings differently, with a view of tabling resolutions for change; and in effect to raise the profile of the church to a more credible and higher levels.

The C & S, still under a century old, can rightly and appropriately change and/or improve on the modality of praising God; and does not need to be apologetic about it. The older denominations are constantly updating their doctrines and homiletics, and the C & S cannot afford to be an exception. Updating and enriching our modalities is certainly our legitimate and spiritual right, to foster the propagation of the Gospel of Christ, and to win more souls for His kingdom.

The significance of Numbers

Certain numbers do carry weight in C & S Epistemology. The church deals with the numbers for Biblical and spiritual reasons and particularly for efficacy of prayers.

One Research student visiting different Pentecostal and Charismatic churches did remark that C & S does many things differently. Of particular interest to her was the way of shouting Hallelujah during the Service and Prayer Meetings. Whereas other denominations shout sporadically, but the C & S follows regulated patterns, sometimes once, thrice or seven times. These numbers amongst others represent different meanings in the C & S liturgy. Regulated numbers also apply to saying prayers, lighting of candles and selection of prayer points. Let us consider a few numbers in turn and briefly explain their meanings.

One Number

One number signifies the unity of the Godhead or the Trinity. As the concept of the Trinity is difficult to understand, it carries a measure of mystery. One in three and three in one is an ongoing debate in Christian Doctrine and believers in the concept only accept its validity as a matter of faith rather than of proof. Some Christians do not even believe in it and they claim rightly that God cannot be divided and opine that the same God is the one who was incarnated and took on human flesh as Jesus the Christ. They also claim that it is the same God who came back after the resurrection as the Holy Spirit. They believe that the name of God is Jesus.

This group of Christians is known and called 'Unitarians' or 'Jesus only' group. Their doctrine is reflected in the way they conduct their practices including baptism by immersion, for instance. Whereas the Trinitarians baptise converts 'in the name of the Father, and of the Son, and of the Holy Spirit' (Matt. 28:19) and dip the candidate in water thrice; the Unitarians in their part perform the same ritual dipping the candidate in water once, 'in the name of Jesus Christ' (Acts 2:38).

Two Number

Two represents the attribute of God as Alpha and Omega. It also represents the nature of Jesus Christ as God in man and man in God. It can be extended to include light and darkness; wrong and right; defeat and victory; failure and success; weeping and rejoicing; great and small; life and death. This number features less than other numbers in C & S Epistemology.

Incidentally, most, if not all African Indigenous Churches were founded by a single Revivalist or Prophet. In the case of Cherubim & Seraphim, it could be said that there were two Co-Founders, Moses Orimolade Tunolase and Christiana Abiodun Akinsowon. This is the Lord's doing. Rather than view the duo as questionable, some positivity could be discerned from it to affirm that 'two heads are better than one.'

Three Number

As explained above, the number three represents the power flowing from the mysterious nature of the Holy Trinity. Three is the number most commonly used in C & S liturgy.

- White candles are usually lit in one, three or seven in worship Service or in Prayer Meetings.

- The Opening Prayer usually consists of three elements: Confession and Forgiveness of sins; Sanctification; Descent of the Holy Spirit.

- Intercession Prayers are usually sectioned into three points of need and said by three different Elders. They are otherwise titled 'Three Peoples' Prayers'.

- Choruses usually in Praise & Worship are sung once, thrice or seven times.

- Shouting of Hallelujahs, Hosanna and Iye are done once, thrice or seven times.

- Sometimes, the same prayer is spiritually directed to be said thrice consecutively, at different times or on three different occasions for emphasis in expectation of efficacy.

- Most of the time, prayers are ended with Amen, Amen, Amen in Jesus' name for the same reason.

- 'The Hour of Prayer' is usually observed at three hourly intervals during long Service or Prayer sessions. The specific hours round the clock being twelve, three, six and nine, day or night.

Four Number

Four and multiples of four are very prominent in the Bible as it is also prominent in the C & S. Almost from prehistoric times, the number four was employed to signify what was solid, what could be touched and felt. Its relationship to the cross (four points) made it an outstanding symbol of wholeness and universality, a symbol which drew all to itself. Without elaborating on the importance of 'four number' let it be sufficient to mention a few.

The Earth has four cardinal directions (or corners as stated in the bible): East and West, North and South (Rev. 7:1). The same scripture also mentions four angels and four winds. The winds represent messengers waiting for the instructions from God for specific purposes. In Ezekiel 37, God commanded the prophet to say to the wind:

Thus saith the Lord God: come from the four winds, O breath, and breathe upon these slain, that they may live (Eze. 37:9)

Scriptures like this become useful in healing prayers particularly when troubled people invariably conclude:

Our bones are dried, and our hope is lost: we are cut off for our parts (Ezek.37:11).

The four winds from the four corners of the Earth can always work wonders for all those who believe in the unfailing power of God.

Five Number

Five is rarely used in C & S Epistemology. In Biblical terms, it represents the five ghastly wounds of Christ on the cross. Reference could be made to the wounds during healing prayers as a reminder that Christ died for us and that:

'He was wounded for our transgressions, he was bruised for our iniquities; the chastisement of our peace was upon him; and with his stripes we are healed (Is.53:5).

Seven Number

- The Seven number is one of the most powerful numbers in C & S Epistemology. The number seven is a heavenly number and one that is a symbol of perfection and eternal life. Since the latter is obsessed with signs and wonders, the number seven is more often used in its liturgy. The following are among the reasons for its use:

- The number seven represents wholeness and perfection in numerology both physically and spiritually. Moses Orimolade completed about seven years in an itinerary mission up and down Nigeria before finally settling down in Lagos to commence a sedentary mission in 1924.

- Seven was symbolic in Israelite and Semitic culture and it communicated a sense of 'fullness' or 'completeness' In Hebrew, the number seven has the same consonants as the word for 'completeness' or 'wholeness'

- God completed the work of creation in six days and rested on the seventh. It is therefore made important to God who hallowed it and declared it a day of rest or the Sabbath of the Lord (Ex. 20:10). The wall of Jericho fell miraculously after marching round the wall seven times. Elisha prescribed washing in River Jordan seven times for Naaman to complete the healing of his leprosy (2 Kings 5).

- In New Testament, the number seven symbolises the unity of the four corners of the Earth (the physical) with the Holy Trinity (the spiritual).

- The number is prominently featured in the Book of Revelation citing seven churches, seven angels, seven seals, seven trumpets and seven stars.

- The Holy Spirit has seven attributes: wisdom, knowledge, understanding, counsel, fortitude, piety and fear of the Lord (Isaiah 11:2).

- Seven candles are always lit on the Altar in C & S Prayer Houses during worship to symbolise the seven fold spirit of God (Rev.4:5), by which Archangel Michael was armed to confront Lucifer (Rev.12:7-10).

Twelve Number

Between Joshua and the first King of Israel, the nation was ruled by twelve judges.

The number twelve is mentioned very often in the Bible especially in the New Testament. Jesus chose twelve apostles deliberately to represent the twelve tribes of Israel. It is said that number twelve is blessed with spirituality and can be seen as a symbol of growth and finding ways to bring deeper meaning to one's life[77]

On the first missionary crusade, Jesus sent out the twelve disciples (Apostles) and gave them power authority over unclean spirits, to cast them out, and to cure every disease and every sickness (Matt. 10). In the second missionary crusade, Jesus was reported as sending seventy disciples with the same mandate (Lk. 10). But was the number of disciples sent seventy or seventy two? Seventy two is a multiple of twelve, which makes it more likely. Seventy is mentioned in some manuscripts of the Alexandrian (such as Codex Sinaiticus) and Caesarean text traditions but seventy two in most other Alaxandrian and Western texts[78]

The twelve number and multiples of twelve feature prominently in the Book of Revelation particularly referring to the twelve tribes of Israel. The number can be powerful in prayers because it is the product of numbers 'three' and 'four' which are themselves powerfully employed in deliverance and healing prayers.

Forty & Four hundred Numbers

Four and multiples of four can rightly be called another number of God. The number forty is mentioned 146 times in the Bible. It generally symbolises a period of testing, trial or probation[79]. Before Cherubim & Seraphim Society came into being, the SON pleaded for forty years; and it took the same forty years for the FATHER to

---

[77] AI (Artifical Intellegence, Google).

[78] Ibid

[79] Ibid

hear and to grant the request, according to the second verse of one C & S hymn (written through vision and revelation):

> *Ogoji odun ni BABA fi gb'ebe, ka le gb'egbe to logo yi dide;*
> *Ogoji odun ni OMO fi bebe, lati d'egbe Serafu yi sile*

Moses Orimolade was about forty years old when he commenced his itinerant missionary journey. Before then, he was involved in local crusades in and around his home town in Ikare. When the Cherubim & Seraphim Society was formally launched in 1925, he prophesied that the Society would expand rapidly throughout Nigeria and Africa and that after forty years, the expansion would go beyond the shores of Africa. That very prophecy was fulfilled in 1965 when the Cherubim & Seraphim was established in London.

Several narratives in the Bible show how important the number forty is to God and it will suffice to mention a few:

In forty days:

- Noah completed building his Arch.
- The earth was flooded by divine intervention.
- The tower of Babel was built.
- Moses' two forty days fast on the Mountain with God.
- The forty days of spying in Canaan.
- Goliath threatened Israel forty days before he was killed by David.
- Elijah fasted forty days as a fugitive to Mount Horeb from the threat of Jezebel.

- Jonah's prophecy that Ninevey would be destroyed in forty days.

- Jesus fasted for forty days and was tempted by the satan in the wilderness.

- Jesus ascended to heaven forty days after his resurrection.

In forty years:

- The Israelites travelled through the wilderness before reaching Canaan.

- Saul, David and Solomon each reigned over Israel for forty years.

In four hundred years:

- Abraham was called in four hundred years after Noah and the flood.

- The Israelites were enslaved in Egypt and nurtured as a nation in preparation for exodus to the promised land.

The above examples show that four, forty and four hundred are paramount numbers in the plan of God to effect changes. The C & S has a big stake in the plan of God as has been pointed out in the foregoing paragraphs. The church has gone through the process of rule by a Supreme Head (Olori) for nearly forty years on a loose confederation type of government. It is hoped that the church will now escalate its status from confederation to central control, whereby each constituent member of the Unification will surrender its sovereignty to the Supreme Head for good. That will be the resurrection of the sleeping giant of African Indigenous Churches worldwide after forty years of confederation of autonomous churches in the Unification.

CHAPTER 11

THE C & S UNDER THE MICROSCOPE

In this day and age, there is no one Christian denomination that can claim perfection or be found blameless theologically and spiritually. All have fallen short of the glory of God. If Jesus should come back today, would he find any church or denomination on earth that is worshipping God in spirit and in truth? Jesus asked the same question by way of prophecy of how changes were bound to develop before His second coming (Lk.18:8). This question then can lead to an honest diagnosis of the strength and weaknesses, threats and opportunities as applied to Cherubim & Seraphim without feeling ashamed about washing our dirty linen in public. This exercise is popularly known as SWOT Analysis. It is mainly used in business to discover the causes of failure and to help with the introduction of new ideas aimed at correcting past errors and improving efficiency and profitability.

The same analysis may also be applied to any church or denomination in order to find ways of improvement in their theologies; and a help to ensure effective delivery of the very purpose of mission and evangelism. This is not to suggest that Cherubim & Seraphim is in any way underperforming. It is only to say that it is not achieving as much as can be expected, considering that it is the first indigenous African Church in Nigeria, and that other indigenous churches have achieved greater heights in mission and evangelism in the same environment and with the same opportunities open to all. Because of this it is reasonable to suggest that a critical diagnosis of the state of health should be conducted on the same line as in secular organisations in order to find feasible remedies capable of rectifying visible deficiencies and to facilitate performance to a higher level than previously attained.

Strengths

There are certain uniqueness in the Cherubim & Seraphim Epistemology that are not common to other denominations. It is, therefore, appropriate to list some of them here as a reminder to our members; and as an offering to non members for greater possible enrichment to their theologies, should they find them useful for their purposes. The outline will indicate positive attributes peculiar to the C & S and which should be embraced and intensified in order to yield greater dividends.

- Efficacy of Prayers -

This is the point at which God intervenes in our lives after asking in prayers. At this point, things change and miracles surface. But what motivates God to intervene in any prayer, if at all? This puzzle is solved in the remarks of Jesus:

First, he said

...this kind goeth not out but by prayer and fasting (Matt. 17:21 KJV).

The key words here are, prayer and fasting. Before the outpouring of the Holy Spirit at Pentecost, the disciples needed these for positive results in their ministry. Before Pentecost, they depended on Jesus when he was still with them physically. They needed to wait for the descent of power from on high as Jesus promised.

After Pentecost, they were endowed with thaumaturgical glows as they experienced the indwelling of the Holy Spirit; and so did not need prayer and fasting before enforcing miracles. The words from their mouths simply came out with power automatically for positive results.

Secondly, Jesus said

Hitherto have ye asked nothing in my name (John 16:24 KJV).

It is only the asking 'in the name of Jesus' that anyone can have a direct line to God for the efficacy of prayers. That is why our prayers end with 'through Jesus Christ, our Lord'. Having said that, it must be emphasised that anointing is a prerequisite as a tool for performance. Indwelling of the Holy Spirit is a must to answered prayers at all times. That is why David prayed:

Cast me not away from thy presence, and take not thy Holy Spirit from me (Ps.51:11).

This is acknowledging that anointing with the Holy Spirit is not permanent but can be withdrawn at the point of violation of the sanctity of the Spirit.

- Faith -

Faith is one of the top emphases Jesus put on his teachings. He always rebuked his disciples for their insufficiency of faith especially whenever he was not in their midst. When they marvelled at the withered fig tree cursed by Jesus, He said unto them:

If ye have faith , and doubt not, ye shall not only do this which is done to the fig tree, but also if ye shall say unto this mountain, Be thou removed, and be thou cast into the sea, it shall be done. And all things, whatsoever ye shall ask in prayer, believing, ye shall receive (Matt. 21:21 KJV).

The emphasis here is the power of faith, the activation of Christian thaumaturgy and the exercise of ethereal gifts. It is interesting to know that whilst academic theology is obsessed with exegetical analysis of Scripture, it has not, and maybe cannot teach anyone on matters of faith and practical spirituality. This is because faith which triggers performative actions is a matter of personal conviction and trust in God, and can best be developed by the individual. The fact is that thaumaturgy is not obsolete and it can be activated, although from the position of 'clean hands and pure hearts' as prescribed by Psalm 24:4. The alternative is the conferment of power from on high through the indwelling of the Holy Spirit as it automatically happened to the disciples on the day of Pentecost.

By faith Elijah challenged the false prophets of Baal when they failed to command fire to burn their offering; as Elijah did successfully after praying to God (I Kings 18: 19-29); by faith Elisha miraculously filled the empty vessels borrowed by a widow with oil to pay her debts and to feed her family (II Kings 4: 1-7); by faith Peter and John healed the lame beggar at the gate of the Temple called Beautiful (Acts 3:1-8); by faith Philip was caught up by the Holy Spirit after baptising the Ethiopian Eunuch

'that the Eunuch saw him no more and he went his way rejoicing but Philip was found in Azotus' (Acts 8:39-40).

The above few examples drawn from both the Old and New Testaments are confirmation that thaumaturgy and ethereal gifts are essential properties of the church, without which the church will look spiritually bereaved, ineffective and dysfunctional. This can be a challenge to churches of every denomination at this end time. The challenge must be taken with fortitude if the church will not be continually perceived as an empty barrel that makes the loudest noise.

-Young Potentials-

The C & S is blessed with young and intelligent youths both male and female. One needs to hear them articulating their assessment of the present state of the church and projecting their proposals for improvement at the Annual General Conference of the church. These youths need to be encouraged and carefully mentored as they are the future of the church. They are conversant with Science and Information Technology and their communication skills are quite relevant to 21st century demands.

However, it cannot be denied that some youths today are too money conscious and whenever there is a proposal for budgetable projects, some of them come forward like opportunist hawks looking for prey, to make money and get rich quick. In other words, it can be observed that some youths have copied bad examples to quickly ask for what material gains they can make from any proposal. All youths, therefore, need to be carefully mentored on certain fundamental rules on ethics and spirituality:

Seek ye first the kingdom of God, and his righteousness; and all these things (including money rewards) shall be added unto you (Matt. 6:33).

Man shall not live by bread alone, but by every word that proceedeth out of the mouth of God (Matt. 4:4)

Sow, grow, tend and nurture to maturity before harvesting (harvesting is beautiful and rewarding but rightly only after the hard work is done) is the natural pattern to life.

Enter ye in at the strait gate: for wide is the gate, and broad is the way, that leadeth to destruction, and many there be which go in thereat. Because strait is the gate, and narrow is the way, which leadeth unto life, and few there be that find it (Matt. 7:13-14 KJV).

The natural life cycle of most popular people in the Bible includes going through hard times and rough patches before prosperity and comfortable times arrive. It is more rewarding to go through the hard time before the easy. This pattern of lifestyle is true of the life of Abraham, Isaac, Jacob, Joseph, David and even Jesus himself. Those who seek to do the short cut and to begin with the easy life can only postpone the hard bit till later, but surely the hard bit cannot be eluded profitably.

But the God of all grace, who hath called us unto his eternal glory by Christ Jesus, after that ye have suffered a while, make you perfect, stablish, strengthen, settle you. (1 Peter 5:10 KJV).

-The Army of Salvation & The Brigade-

The activities of the Youths in C & S in this regard have been described in a previous chapter as an added value to our liturgy. Besides posing beautiful cosmetics to the quality of worship, their activities also present challenges to the youths as a motivator to developing their potentials for possible careers in their countries' National Armies.

Military disciplines would have become their second nature and apart from seeking careers in the Armed Forces, training in disciplines will always be found useful in their personal and domestic endeavours.

-Doers of the Word-

Cherubim & Seraphim of whatever persuasion is never short of supply of aspirants for high office in our hierarchy. One needs to attend an Ordination Service in C & S to see a huge number of members offering themselves, or are selected to be anointed. Most ordinands would have gone through a series of induction sessions before their anointing. That can be a good sign of readiness to contribute to the work of the Gospel with the expectation of a high reward from above.

But whoso looketh into the perfect law of liberty, and continueth therein, he being not a forgetful hearer, but a doer of the work, this man shall be blessed in his deed (James 1:25 KJV).

-Freely ye receive, freely give-

Except in larger congregations where a few office holders are remunerated, most workers in C & S including Pastors and Ministers-in-Charge offer their services free as most of them earn their living from secular sources. In the larger congregations, the demand for ecclesiastical services becomes complex and requires greater attention. Full time workers, therefore, become inevitable and such workers must essentially be remunerated. Unremunerated workers in the church are similar to the Roman Catholic system where priests are unwaged but their expenses met by the church. Where and when such services are given voluntarily from a willing heart, there can be great reward in heaven. In the C & S Epistemology, ordination vows forbid charging for prayers and elements used, such as candles, oil and water. Any charging for these services as described will therefore be seen as a deviant, and not representative of C & S Epistemology.

-Consecration & Exorcism-

On the purchase of property for living or for business, members usually call on Elders for consecration of the premises for safety and prosperity. Consecration also covers properties infested with unclean spirits where the dwellers live in fear and insecurity. The process involves conducting short Prayers which may include appropriate songs, reading from the Scriptures and relevant prayers for deliverance from fear, insecurity, protection, healing and prosperity. One, three or seven candles are lit; incense burnt and flicked through the property; consecrated water is sprinkled at the four corners of each room and also at doorways leading to the house. The consecration is then concluded with songs and prayers of thanksgiving for God's faithfulness.

-Founders' Legacy-

The legacy of the blessings bestowed on Abraham, Isaac and Jacob are still working in the lives of the Jews anywhere they live and work till today. The covenant of God with Abraham still remains with the Jews till today. Whatever they lay their hands on will always result in prosperity because of their forefathers' legacy. Even though they live in the midst of their enemies, they still overcome all hatred and attacks on them, especially from their neighbours.

In the same way, the legacy of the special ethereal gifts and thaumaturgy with which Orimolade was blessed; and the prophetic gifts of visions and revelations with which Abiodun was blessed still remain in the lives of Cherubim & Seraphim till today. Signs and Wonders have not ceased and glory be to God that evidence can be spotted albeit on a smaller level than expected. Other Christian denominations may try to emulate the divine gifts characteristic of the C & S but apparently, counterfeits can never be compared with originals. The Founders' legacies will always be evident in the lives of practitioners that adhere strictly to C & S Epistemology; but not necessarily on the imposters. Unfortunately, the imposters are in the majority today in C & S and they are dangerously defiling the legacy of the Founders of the church. It is evident that many 'wolves' have invaded the church but appear in sheep's clothing. The consolation is that at harvest time, the goats shall be separated from the sheep.

Weaknesses

In practically every Christian denomination, there are weaknesses that cannot be denied and which should be outed in order to find ways and means of eradicating them and to attain good governance and robust theology. The Cherubim & Seraphim is not an exception to the need of re-engineering without being apologetic, and the following, therefore, should be exposed with the hope that the exposition would trigger repentance and repositioning:

-Schism-

In Christianity, schism occurs when a single religious body divides and becomes two or more separate religious bodies. A split can be violent or nonviolent but results in at least one of the newly created bodies considering itself distinct from the other. The Cherubim & Seraphim Society suffered from this evil when in 1929 the successful partnership between Orimolade and Abiodun was broken. The latter left Orimolade to register her own faction as the Cherubim & Seraphim Society, the name that was pronounced for the Society in 1925. As Orimolade could not legally share the same name after this registration, his own Section required a new name. Subsequently, his wing of Cherubim & Seraphim was named the Eternal Sacred Order. Other divisions followed shortly after until five distinct major Sections emerged namely:

- Eternal Sacred Order of Cherubim & Seraphim
- Cherubim & Seraphim Society
- Praying Band of Cherubim & Seraphim
- Sacred Cherubim & Seraphim and
- The Holy Order of Cherubim & Seraphim Movement.

Out of these five major churches, other separations have developed to further make the profile of the church less credible. Most of the emerging Sections have anointed their Sectional Heads as Baba Aladura, the rank held by Moses Orimolade. The exception is the Sacred Cherubim & Seraphim which chose to anoint its Sectional Head as Baba Alakoso, as a mark of respect for Moses Orimolade. In Cherubim & Seraphim today, many Sectional Heads adopt titles such as Baba Aladura, Archbishop, Primate, General Overseer or General Leader, Founder and such other titles that suit their appetites.

These vulgar profiles need to be outed in order for members to see themselves as outsiders see them. Perhaps, some goodness can result from rethinking our theologies and seek ways and means of repackaging our profiles to a level that can command respect internally and externally. To repackage successfully requires a good measure of humility and fear of God; the awareness that earthly glories do not, and cannot earn any credit towards salvation and eternity.

As the church is fast approaching celebration of its centenary year, it is a time to take the message of God seriously and repent:

If my people, which are called by my name, shall humble themselves, and pray, and seek my face, and turn from their wicked ways; then will I hear from heaven, and will forgive their sin, and will heal their land (2Chro. 7:14 KJV).

And then if convinced of the need for a change to resort to the penitent route:

Let the priests, the ministers of the Lord, weep between the porch and the altar, and let them say, Spare thy people, O Lord, and give not thine heritage to reproach, that the heathen should rule over them; wherefore should they say among the people, where is their God?(Joel 2:17 KJV).

Most of the Sectional Heads today are innocent especially when they are not among the first generation of breakaways. But yet they have a major part to play in the repentance process. In humility, solutions can be found to correct the past mistakes.

-Leadership, Education & Training-

It can be an understatement to assert that education and training can no longer be ignored as necessary for ministry and leadership in this twenty-first century. Gone are the days when ministers of the Gospel only paid lip service to education but claim that they have received their education at the cross, where the Holy Spirit is the Teacher. Such a claim could be valid in the twentieth century but not in the twenty-first as education has gone to higher levels amongst the recipients of the Gospel message. To ignore this shift in higher education differentials is tantamount to putting 'new wines in old wine skins'. This is one of the reasons why some C & S youths have defected to other denominations that they consider more relevant to their spiritual needs. It has, therefore, become a serious issue that needs to be addressed.

Communication skills have developed and many old people are now IT (Information Technology) friendly even if, as it were, the majority of the older members are still resisting change and fail to move along with time. Such resistance apparently caused problems for many of the old people, particularly during the Covid-19 pandemic which is still lingering on. It is therefore reasonable to argue in favour of combining spiritual gifts/ anointing with education (at higher or professional level) and training as vitally crucial to success in ecclesiology, missiology and evangelism in these times. Churches which have adapted to the inevitable changes have moved forward in development, whilst leaving behind those that prefer to remain conservative and hence, remain stagnant.

-Refresher Courses-

The foregoing has put emphasis on Education. Training is the second component to any successful ministry. Those ministers and leaders who did not have the advantage of higher education but are well versed in ministerial and leadership attributes can always accept training and retraining in order to acquire up-to-date communication skills with which they can effectively articulate their wisdom with the younger generations. This can be the difficult part of putting right what has gone wrong in our system. It requires a good measure of humility which cannot be easily enforced, but before God all things are possible. Repentance, humility, tolerance, endurance and persistence are the necessary tools capable of delivering the required results.

It should be remembered that not all highly educated people are, ipso facto, leadership material; and that screening process needs to be in place to select the right candidates for the right positions. Questions of spiritual maturity, personality, character, integrity, respectability, humility and adaptability, amongst others are vital to the screening process.

-Autonomy & Stand Alone Syndrome-

As if the first split of Cherubim & Seraphim Society in 1929 was not sad enough, subsequent other splits followed with each new split operating in isolation autonomously and appointing their Spiritual Heads as Baba Aladuras. The number of autonomous C & S churches has now grown to around 100 even though the church is still under 100 years old! The unbecoming practice of splitting has effectively replaced the original foundation of church planting headed by Captain Abiodun who, through her energetic and charismatic gifts led the planting of many branches outside of Lagos with the instruction of Moses Orimolade as Leader. As a result of Abiodun's successful church planting, Orimolade accorded her the title of 'Captain' which was the only title she held till her transition into glory. If this method of expanding the horizons of the church has been followed till today, the question of splitting from one another and of autonomy would not have arisen. On the other hand, if only church planting had been the only way of expanding the church, the C & S perhaps may not have been as numerous as it is today. The important factor to consider is that quality will always be more important than quantity in most respects. Unity (which strengthens) will always be more valued than disunity (that weakens).

It is a fact of nature that the pulling together and corporate deployment of resources will always achieve greater results than the aggregate of individual efforts put together. It is called

- Unity is Strength
- United we stand, divided we fall
- Economies of scale and Synergy

The quality and benefit of unity can stand out under two obvious scenarios. First, in the event of any crisis, it is usually the combined effort of the community that can defend a victim from the attack of a predator. Most of the time a single defence would normally end up in defeat. Secondly, in the event of any possible opportunities arising, again it is the combined effort of the community that can make possible what proves to be impossible for a single member of the community. These two scenarios affirm that 'united we stand, divided we fall'. Investing in unity (stability) is a matter of wisdom. On the other hand, investing in individuality may indicate a lack of sufficient wisdom. There will usually be some short term advantage in a 'stand alone' or selfish attitude, but such a stand can become regrettable in the longer term when united efforts begin to yield greater dividends. These choices are not imperative with spirituality per se, but they have a lot to do with wisdom and economic stability. The latter can be found crucial to the health of the former.

'Synergy' is the concept that the value and performance of two companies combined will be greater than the sum of the separate individual parts. It is sometimes described as 2 + 2 = 5. which is arithmetically incorrect but economically valid. It is like turning ordinary into extraordinary. It is made possible when communities embrace unity. It is spiritually valid and answers the prayer of Jesus '*Holy Father keep through thine own name those whom thou hast given me, that they may be one, as we are*' *(John 17:11)*. As in any Christian marriage both parties are to overcome their differences (personality types, backgrounds, values etc.) and be humble enough to compromise, forgive and submit to one another as the spirit leads. It takes purposeful commitment and hard work by all parties in remembering the covenant made before the Lord , open communication and the humility to submit to Christ's will, to achieve peace and retain love in such a union.

-Squabble for Power and Positions—

The sons of Zebedee syndrome has infected the C & S and humility has been set aside in the service of God. James and John, either by themselves or by their mother, requested that Jesus should allow one of them to sit on his right, and the other on the left hand-side in his kingdom. Jesus rebuked them for such inordinate ambition and explained to them that the positions they sought after had been predetermined and not available for negotiation. This explanation seems to have been ignored or snubbed by most members and especially Elders of the C & S. The worrying trend of thought is that the grander the titles they hold and the higher their profiles, the nearer to paradise they would be perceived to be! As a result, they would go to any length of causing trouble and discomfort to fellow members in order to attain self-glorification. Paul did warn people of pride and of humility:

Every man that is among you, not to think of himself more highly than he ought to think; but to think soberly, according as God hath dealt to every man the measure of faith (Rom. 12:5).

But instead to,

Be kindly affectioned one to another with brotherly love, in honour preferring one another (Rom. 12:10).

-Unnecessary Ordination Grades-

At the beginning of the church, there was nothing like Ordination of anybody and apart from the Co-Founders, everybody else remained a Brother or a Sister. As Co-Founders, Orimolade was called Baba Aladura and Abiodun was called Captain. Both were nicknames and never a formal ordination rooted. At some stage in the history of the church, the Ephesian model of ministry was adopted:

And he gave some, apostles; and some prophets; and some, evangelists; and some pastors and teachers (Eph.4:11).

According to Paul, the above titles were given by Jesus to ministers of the Gospel after his ascension. Before his ascension, the twelve were simply called 'Apostles' without any superlative adjective. All were equal. Not even Peter (the rock on which the church was built), nor James and John who, along with Peter were the three chosen to follow Jesus on special occasions were called 'Senior Apostles' as it would have been expected. It should be noted that he (Jesus) did not give 'Senior'; 'Junior'; 'Superintendent' or any other superlative adjective to the five-hierarchy as outlined above. The five-hierarchy has now become ten or more as the superlative adjectives continue to expand.

The result is that the humility which Jesus taught and did particularly emphasise, has been overturned and bastardised in our midst. If we should remember Jesus and his teachings especially on humility, we surely need repentance. Repentance can start by dropping all unnecessary titles we have given ourselves because they are the principal contributory factors leading to unhealthy rivalry, squabble for power and positions.

How can we effectively propagate the Gospel of Christ with these impediments hanging on our shoulders? Evidence has shown that many Ordination ceremonies have triggered dissensions, strife and separations. Those who felt cheated for not being accorded their expected ordination grades or levels very often leave the particular church or congregation and join another. Some even go further to establish their own separate branch and accord themselves with questionable titles. Regrettably, it has become commonplace in C & S that anyone, irrespective of knowledge, training or qualification can move out of one congregation to establish another without fear or restriction.

-White Robing?-

The principal purpose of robbing in white was to enforce uniformity in an egalitarian spirit, so that no one member can be seen as superior to another. That was how Jesus related to his disciples. It was introduced as a uniform such as in a Football Team. Even in the latter scenario, the Team Captain always wears a 'hand band' to distinguish him from the rest. The intention in the C & S setting was even not to identify any Captain or Leader, but to see all members as one without any hand band. That was why Judas had to distinguish Jesus at his arrest by kissing him. This purpose has been heavily eroded in different ways in the C & S.

First, different colours have been introduced to distinguish between holders of low and high office. At the beginning, this distinction was limited to notable Elders, but now it looks like no member can be stopped from choosing what colour to wear. There is no law and order in place to regulate anything.

Second, for those who adhere to white colour, different quality fabrics are used without questioning. Poplin, Silk, Damask, Lace, even see-through materials are becoming common as in a fashion parade! Introduction of these varieties have effectively rubbished the initial purpose of robbing in white.

A further deviation is how especially in the women fold, head gear and particularly prayer gowns either in white or in any other colour are tailored. Some prayer gowns are built in straight loose format looking like anybody else's whilst some are built to fit the exact shape of the wearer thus attracting undue attention. It is reasonable to remember that whenever an ordinary becomes extraordinary it is not difficult to deduce that what is normal has become abnormal.

These scenarios may be acceptable in social environments but never in the spiritual.

Opportunities

There are several opportunities open to the church if repentance is taken seriously and a quick shift is made possible from 'autonomy and isolationism' (where we are presently) into unity and consolidation (which is always the recipe for growth and progress). The church can best serve the community from the position of strength than from the position of weakness. It is an understatement to remind everyone that division and isolationism give rise to weakness; but united front and consolidation give rise to strength. Let us consider some opportunities that the church has missed.

-Laudable Projects-

Pooling together of resources by the small units can result in establishing Full Time Administrative Centres from where strategies can best be operative and implemented. Single churches or congregations cannot usually afford to set up fully staffed Administrative Centres. It should be noted that without such Centres, growth and progress would be drastically impeded. An example is the failure of the church to compete with other denominations in Nigeria to build a University in the name of Cherubim & Seraphim. Other denominations, though younger by establishment, have succeeded because they are united and not given to autonomy and isolationism. It is difficult to fault the idea that unity is strength.

Smaller and younger denominations, it should be noted, have also established community based projects including:

- Housing for homeless people
- Day Centres for social and relaxation opportunities for old age people

- Permanent accommodation for old age pensioners, widows and widowers

- Supplementary education for youths who cannot catch up at School or College

- Skill development for youths not academically gifted

- Induction and interview skills for the unemployed

- Rehabilitation initiatives for ex prisoners

- Establishment of Hospitals for the sick

- Under School Nurseries to release young mothers for gainful employments

These and other laudable projects are included in the assignments of the Gospel of Christ. United and strong Christian denominations are able to provide many of these, but how many of them have the C & S done?

-Money making Projects-

The above projects cannot all be funded from church collections and thanksgiving offerings. Money making projects will always fill the gap. Research can be carried out to determine low risk and high earning projects like investment in:

- Starting and running restaurants

- Extra curriculum evening schools

- Building and running Reception Centres for various occasions

- Running Grocery Stores and possibly graduating into Supermarkets
- Haulage and Delivery Services
- Building and running Bakeries with C & S logo on the wrappings
- Establish C & S Car Washing Business
- Etc.

These projects would require investment in initial and running costs which only united and financially strong organisations can provide. Although money making projects are not the primary objective of religious organisations, they can be the very essential vehicles on which religious functions can thrive. They offer opportunities to make the organisation function smoothly.

If the church grows stronger and financially viable, and if it succeeds in and runs one or more of these projects, it will not only succeed in providing essential services to the community at large; it will also be able to cater for its own members in job opportunities. It will be a win-win scenario for all and the requirements of the Gospel would have been fulfilled. However, the operating practices must distinguish themselves from those commonly found in the secular world. Great care must be taken to establish structures and systems of transparency and accountability, to overcome the trust deficit which is likely to rear its head, once money starts to emerge from the businesses. A level of professionalism and openness on progress will encourage members to invest without uncomfortable questions or accusations emerging in the corridors.

Threats

Possible threats to the Cherubim & Seraphim Church will be determined by its strength to withstand the test of credibility as a Christian denomination should external influences especially in different countries decide to attack or to restrict the activities of the church. Such interference has been tried in Nigeria when the State Government in Kwara State (and maybe in other States) proposed to regulate the appointment of Trustees of Christian Churches and Schools, with a view to gain control of all Christian Churches and Schools. The School Uniform of Christian Schools was also interfered with as the idea of single uniform was challenged. Perhaps the State Proposals were shelved or suspended because of the strength of the Christian churches in the State presenting a united front to object. This is one of the virtues of unity as opposed to autonomy and fragmentation of organisations. Weak organisations always fall prey to predators at the time of crisis but strong organisations always survive. Survival is a function of unity and in turn, unity is the necessity to attain strength. There is no alternative.

-Relegation Possibilities-

Whether we admit it or not, running a church is somewhat similar to running a Football Club. The performance of FCs is monitored and evaluated on a regular basis and the Football Association does regular grading of the different Clubs in the Association. The gradings are based on individual performance of the Clubs especially in the number of goals scored over a period of time. The ambition of each Club is always to be numbered in the Premier League. It is seen as a pride to be numbered among the Premier League and a failure if not included. Similarly, churches or denominations can be subject to such gradings and frequent relegations can always lead to extinction.

That is why each player whether in football or in a church scenario should always strive to put up the best performance at all times. Any player found to underperform will definitely drift into relegation and probably to eventual extinction. In the case of the C&S church which is our concern in this book, extinction can be imminent if youths relegate the C&S and by essentially drifting away from the church making leadership succession difficult. The result could be the gradual shrinking of the church as membership declines. Decline in membership and subsequent reduction in income would lead to the church not being viable. As expenditures begin to rise higher than income, closure and eventual extinction will become imminent.

CHAPTER 12

CONCLUSIONS

It would be seen that throughout the pages of this book that the AICs have variously developed from unplanned backgrounds and as the churches grow, they pick up pieces of practices and formulate doctrines, as they look critically at contemporary church doctrines. It cannot be argued that the Cherubim & Seraphim Church today in her various traditions is not exactly what it used to be in the days of the Founders and in her formative years. It is unclear when ministerial modality as found in Ephesian 4 was adopted in the C & S church. Most certainly, there was no ordination of Elders into the ranks of Teachers, Pastors, Evangelists, Prophets and Apostles in the early days of the church. Moses Orimolade himself was never called a prophet nor was he called an apostle, but simply as Baba Aladura, meaning the father of the church whose passion was to pray for deliverance and healing of those who approached him for help.

No one church among the AICs can claim to be independent of others in terms of doctrine as it would be seen that the churches share greater commonalities in practice and doctrine than few other characteristics that separate them. What separates the churches would simply be matters of understanding and interpretation of Scripture, apart from the desire of some who simply want to be different and autonomous from other traditions. It can be seen that the mainstream and orthodox churches, by virtue of their longevity provide a benchmark against which the younger churches like the AICs compare and contrast their profiles; and

Conclusions

from which they develop their own doctrines and practices which attract updating from time to time as the Spirit directs.

Examples are African churches that applied for membership of the World Council of Churches without a recognisable statement of doctrine. Such churches had to go back to write or rewrite their doctrines which essentially must include their belief in the concept of Trinity. The latter is an important requisite for admission to membership but unknown to most AIC applicants. This confirms that matters of doctrine are not particularly of primary importance to most AICs. The calling to preaching the Gospel of Christ and the quest for thaumaturgy and ethereal gifts are more important and form the genesis of most of the churches.

This kind of analysis applies only to the older AICs such as the Cherubim & Seraphim and the Apostolics in Nigeria. The other newer AICs such as the Church of the Lord Aladura, the Celestial Church of Christ, the 'Winners' group, the Redeemed Christian Church of God and other prosperity gospellers have their own separate visions of what they wanted to achieve, and have developed strategies to achieve their visions. It can be said that whereas the older AICs have grown from unplanned, illiterate or semi literate and prophetic backgrounds, the newer AICs on the other hand, have developed from informed backgrounds and have deliberately deviated from the ethos of the older ones, overthrew the undesirable taboos particularly drawn from Old Testament tenets, not because they are not scripturally valid , but because principally in their view, they are no longer relevant to modern Christian life.

It is reasonable to assume that churches with that kind of mindset can be described as populist and compromising religious truths to suit secular priorities. It is also reasonable to assert that as Jesus did not come to destroy tenets of the Old Testament but actually to fulfil them; so it is reasonable to believe that Christian Scripture actually derives from the Old Testament; and that the New Testament is only the fulfilment of the Old. This idiom is in conformity with the C & S Epistemology. In his Sermon on the mount, Jesus did warn:

Think not that I am come to destroy the law, or the prophets; I am not come to destroy, but to fulfil. For verily I say unto you, till heaven and earth pass, one jot or one tittle shall in no wise pass from the law, till all be fulfilled. Whosoever therefore shall break one of these least commandments, and shall teach men so, he shall be called the least in the kingdom of heaven; but whosoever shall do and teach them, the same shall be called great in the kingdom of heaven (Matt. 5:17-19).

The Cherubim & Seraphim was popular, admired and respected as a formidable revival movement spiritually equipped to correct ecclesiastical and missional inadequacies in Nigeria during the 1920s but unfortunately now seems to have degenerated into a sort of pariah status ecumenically (to the extent that people question the C&S Christian status). It should be recognised that the validity of its epistemology is still intact. If adulteration of the latter is cleansed and somehow removed, and if genuine players in its ethos are opportune to go back to basics, then it would definitely be acknowledged that the C & S Epistemology is the best gift of God to Christianity globally and for the salvation of men on earth.

There must be, therefore, a programmed cleansing crusade in place into which all Sectors of the church must participate. It is then, and only then that the church will regain its old glory to play its part in the preparation for eternity. If Jesus must return to the faithful in a glorious Rapture as prophesied and expected, then every believer must play their part in propagating the Gospel to all corners of

Conclusions

the earth. True propagation cannot be done except in spirit and in truth. The C & S cannot participate fully in this propagation until it can embrace full scale repentance in humility. There must be a cleansing crusade and exorcism of anti-Christ presence in the fold. Cherubim & Seraphim Epistemology must be restored. A 'Do nothing' strategy cannot be an option. Stagnation can no longer be tolerated. There must be Reformation.

The cry for Reformation is not new. Concerned Seraphs have tabled several Resolutions at the recent Annual General Conferences of the church covering the obstacles to growth and progress as outlined above but implementation has been either too slow or completely ignored. It is obvious that Sectional Heads or Baba Aladuras have major roles to play in the implementation of Conference Resolutions. They are the chief Agents for implementation. The question should be asked:

Who is blocking implementation of Conference Resolutions?

Jesus asked the same question and each disciple nervously asked him back:

Lord, is it I? (Matt, 26:22)

Let our Sectional Heads or Baba Aladuras ask themselves the same question.

Judas was spiritually ignorant of the implication of his actions, and despite the fact that Jesus answered him:

Thou hast said (Matt. 26:25)

He still went ahead to betray his Lord, thinking that Jesus was more than capable of defending himself and that the Authorities who wanted to arrest him would end up as fools. He was wrong. Jesus did not want to defend himself. Self defence would have meant an obstacle to his mission to take away the sins of the world, which he accomplished on the cross. We must all pray daily for our Leaders and Baba Aladuras that:

- They will not be wrong.
- They will take the right steps towards building a stronger Unification.
- They will not embrace short term advantage to the detriment of the longer term.
- They will become joint heirs with Christ in his kingdom.
- It will be well for them, so that it can be well for us too.
- Cherubim & Seraphim Church, the sleeping giant, will rise again and prosper.
- The reign of Christ on earth will begin. Glory be to the name of the Lord.

The Effects of Schism in the C & S

God works in mysterious ways in order to perform His wonders. It is certain that the ambition of true Seraphs is that the church should grow and multiply as they believe it is so commanded in heaven. The wonderful aspect of the desired ambition is to be found in the methodology of achieving growth and multiplication. There are two obvious methods. Growth through church planting and growth through schism and division. Let us consider the merits and demerits of both.

Church planting is honest and truthful but not cheap to achieve. It requires resources that can always be scarce and churches are always slow to go that route. It can best be achieved as and when resources surplus to requirement become available. The resources include manpower and finance. Manpower calls for full time or part time training at high cost and finance is not easy to accumulate. Churches that wait for this noble method are always slow in mission and evangelism. This method is uncommon in the C & S.

The alternative, though not always ideal, is to divide and multiply. Multiplication through division is always risky and generally evil. It is risky because it involves the separatist abandoning his comfort zone and going into the wilderness very often with inadequate resources—spiritual maturity, manpower and finance. Unfortunately, this method is very common in the C & S. Incidentally, this method obviously accounts for the phenomenal growth of the church globally today.

Should we therefore congratulate the church for the growth based on division? God forbid. It cannot be a matter for congratulations nor can it be for condemnation. In schism and division, enmity between factions is fostered whilst harmony of purpose and uniformity of doctrine are hampered. It creates damaged relationships that are always difficult to repair. But God works in mysterious ways in order to perform his wonders. What is difficult for men is not necessarily difficult for God before whom all things are possible.

The reason for optimism is that C & S emerged from humble beginnings and ill equipped for mission and evangelism. The mystery in the expansion of the church is that with little or no resources, the church is growing faster than can be ordinarily expected from churches of its calibre. The expansion in the church has come out of personal financial sacrifices that would not have been possible voluntarily, should the church be asking for monetary contributions. In separating from one another, several differences in worship and liturgy including dress codes have been introduced by the progenitors. Different models of being Cherubim and Seraphim have emerged over the years. The problem is now on how to bridge the spiritual and organisational gaps that have been created through schism and division.

First and perhaps the most important is the lack of spiritual grooming in line with the original pattern of Christ and through discipleship has contributed to a lack of submission to one another, as laid out by the C&S founders Baba Aladura Moses Orimolade and Captain Abiodun. Distinguishing between those that draw solely on the power of God through the name of Jesus Christ and imposters that draw from other sources, under the guise of C&S is fundamental to the restoration of glory to the church. Secondly our systems, our codes of practice, our dress codes and our times of worship and prayer which hitherto have been found incoherent, all need to be harmonised such that what obtains in any one location should be the same in every other. Such is the norm across many Christian denominations. That is the first problem to be solved.

The third is the consolidating of our resources for greater exploits. Opportunities have arisen to showcase the strength of the church but unfortunately many have been lost because our resources, especially financial, have been scattered into different segmental controls. If all assets of the church had been pooled together and

Conclusions

consolidated, it would have been easy for the church to build universities, hospitals, mission homes like for old people, orphans, homeless people, rehabilitation centres, fully staffed Administrative Centres necessary for the smooth running of the church; and such other laudable projects that have been achieved by several contemporary and younger denominations.

Cherubim & Seraphim as a church has been disappointed for the reason of being subdued into schism and division over many years. But if it is a true saying that 'every disappointment is a blessing from God' then the church will come to appreciate God for the splits in the church; which led to pseudo expansion but which did not remain divided forever. The subsequent pseudo expansion will hopefully convert to a huge blessing (when the present 'confederation' type of church government would have turned into a 'central' type). Then the church will be bold to proclaim the glory of God who would have turned our shame into glory. It would have been very difficult to attain the same level of expansion with the kind of background from which the church evolved: illiterate, poor, unstructured, unplanned and ill equipped!

Although one prophetic C & S song claims:

There's command from the Court of Heaven, that this Band must multiply;

There's command from the Court of Heaven, to grow from strength to strength;

Because of the poor background from which the church emerged, it is difficult to imagine that it could 'multiply and grow from strength to strength' without the planning and financial resources required for church planting. Hence, 'split and multiply' became convenient to achieve the 'commands'.

Good News

The progenitors of schism in the C & S should be assured that the past belongs to the past and there is no condemnation for past mistakes. As long as there is life, there is hope for repair work to be set in motion. Now is the time, before the church celebrates its centenary year in 2025 that the different divisions come together to sing from the same song sheet: One Lord, One Faith, One Baptism. In repentance, every Seraph should be prepared to sing:

All to Jesus I surrender, all to Him I freely give;
Worldly pleasures, all forsaken, take me, Jesus, take me now.

The End Time is at hand and the faithful of the Lord must not be caught unprepared. What we are holding and protecting as too precious and reluctant to release will, in the end, be controlled and enjoyed by those who have not worked for them! It is a fact of life when one's life comes to an end. It is more blessed to invest our achievements, our gifts, our skills, our trophies, our glories, our treasures and everything we hold as precious, all in the projects which can glorify the name of the Lord; than to invest them in flimsy and perishable ventures that will finally fade away with the world.

After the ascension of our Lord, the disciples decided to pool their resources together so that provision could be made available for all irrespective of individual means. Ananias and his wife, Sapphira fell foul of the agreement by keeping part of the proceeds of their sold property; and subsequently lost their lives. We need to pool our resources together for greater exploits and we need to be honest

Conclusions

about it. Honesty about doing the right has great rewards and default can end in disaster. Let everyone beware of taking the right decisions.

The good news waiting to be announced will be the time when all Sections of the church will come together courageously and pool their resources together for the common good. The Section Heads like Baba Aladuras, Primates, General Leaders or General Overseers, Alakosos and any other Spiritual Head who have worked very hard to build their empires are now opportune to take the courage to surrender their sovereignty to a single Supreme Head (Olori) for the common good; whilst still retaining their respective titles and privileges. That would be the way of the cross which, thank God, has led to victory over death and the grave; and has ushered in the glorious beauty of the resurrection. The chorus of the hymn 'On a hill far away' goes:

So I'll cherish the old rugged cross, till my trophies at last I lay down
I will cling to the old rugged cross, and exchange it someday for a crown.

The ultimate in our religion and faith is to receive the crown of glory when Christ will resume his reign all over the world, where the faithful will reign with him in his kingdom. Such will be the portion of our Sectional Heads who, meanwhile, would have surrendered their sovereignty (and titles) to their Supreme Head in order for each Head to exchange it for a crown. Jesus reminds us:

For what is a man profited, if he shall gain the whole world, and lose his own soul? Or what shall a man give in exchange for his soul? (Matt. 16:26).

Cherubim & Seraphim Church should not be too ashamed nor continue to feel guilty of its past profile. The previous chapters in this book putting the church under the microscope has revealed much about the woes of the church and has taught us to admit that:

To everything there is a season, and a time to every purpose under the heaven (Eccl.3:1)

For Cherubim & Seraphim Church,

- There is a time to agree and a time to disagree
- There is a time to be one body and a time to separate into autonomous bodies
- There is a time to be ashamed of our performance and there is a time to be proud of it
- There is a time to be adamant, notwithstanding and there is a time to repent
- There is a time to enjoy separatism and be weak in schism
- But there is a time to repent, unite and be strong again.

Before the church celebrates its centenary year (2025), it is time to abandon division, weakness and shame, and to become more pro-active, amalgamate and regain old glories for greater exploits for the effective propagation of the Gospel of Christ. It is then and only then that C & S can adequately compete in contemporary missiology.

Looking back on the SWOT analysis in the previous chapter has opened up the opportunity to re-evaluate its mission, correct past errors and positively look forward, to reposition the church on a new profile to which all Seraphs will be proud to belong; and begin to enjoy a fresh fulfilment, to which other Christians will say '.it can only be God'.

BIBLIOGRAPHY

Adegoke, John O, Models of Mission: MA Assignment Module 403, 2005 *How central is prayer for healing in the mission of African Indigenous Churches?* (Unpublished)

Adegoke, John O, Pneumatology of Mission, MA Assignment Module 402.1 2005 *Discuss the significance of the Day of Pentecost both in its New Testament Setting and in modern Pentecostal missiology.* (Unpublished)

Ayegboyin, Deji & Ishola, S, Ademola: *African Indigenous Churches* Lagos, Greater Heights Publications 1997.

Barrett, David: *in Schism and Renewal in Modern Africa*, Nairobi, OUP 1968.

Beaumont, Mark, *MA Module 403*, BCC Lecture Note 6 2003

Daniel, Inus, *Quest for belonging*, Harare, Manbo Press 1987

Daniel, Inus, *Zionism and faith healing in Rhodesia*, The Hague, Mouton 1970

Dolvo, Elon: *Exchange, Journal of Missiological and Ecumenical Research,* Vol33(2004).

Dorr, Donald: *Mission in today's world*, Co Dublin, The Columba Press. 2000

Dunn, James D. G.: *Baptism in the Holy Spirit,* London SCM 1973

Bibliography

Fakeye, G O & Fabiyi, E A, *TENETS OF FAITH for C & S Council of Churches Worldwide,* Supreme Press Limited, Lagos, 1990

Gerloff, Roswith J. H: *A Plea for Black British Theologies*, Frankfurt Main, Peter Lang 1991.

Hayward, V. E. W.: *African Independent Church Movements*, London, Edinburgh, House Press, 1963.

Harris, Hermion, *Yoruba in Diaspora, An African Church in London.* Pelgrave Macmillan, 2006.

Idowu, Bolaji: *Olodumare, God in Yoruba Belief,* London, Longmans 1962

Jenkins, Philip, *The Next Christiandom, The coming of Global Christianity,* Oxford. OUP 2002.

Ludwig, Frieder: Journal of Religion in Africa. 23(4).

MacRobert, Iain: *Black Roots and White Racism of Early Pentecosgalism in the USA* Basingstoke, Macmillan 1988

Mazibuko, B. A: *Mission is crossing Barriers, ed. Roswith Gerloff,* Cluster Publications, 2003.

McGavran, D. A: *(Ed) Church Growth and Christian Mission,* New York, Harper & Row. 1965

Milingo, E: *The World in Between, Christian Healing and the Struggle for Spiritual Survival.* London C. Hurst & Co. (Publishers) Ltd. 1984.

Ndiokwere, Nathaniel: *Prophecy and Revelation*, London SPCK, 1981

Newbigin, Leslie: *The Gospel in a Plural Society*, London, SPCK, 1992.

O hOgain, Daithi, *The Sacred Isle: Belief and Religion in Pre-Christian Ireland*, Cork, Collins Press, 1999.

Omoyajowo, Akin J, *An African Expression of Christianity*, ed Basil Moore in Black Theology, London, C. Hurst & Company 1973

Omoyajowo, Akin J, *Cherubim and Seraphim, The History of an African Independent Church*, New York, London, Lagos, Enugu, NOK Publishers International 1982.

Oosthuizen G.C: *Post-Christianity in Africa – A theological and anthropological Study*. London, C. Hurst & Co. 1968.

Osun, Chris: *Encountering of Aladura Spirituality in Britain*, (unpublished). 1981.

Peel, J.D.Y: ***Aladura****: A Religious Movement among the Yoruba*, London OUP 1968

Pretorius, H. L.: *Ethiopia stretches out her hand unto God*, Pretoria, University of Pretoria, 1993

Pruitt, Raymond M: *Foundamentals of the faith*, Cleveland, White Wing Publishing 2000.

Slipper, Callan, Grove Books: '*Enriched by the Other: a spiritual guide to receptive ecumenism*'

Bibliography

Sundkler, Bengt: *The Bantu Prophets in South Africa*, London, Lutterworth Press 1961

Turner, H.W.: *'A typology for African religious movements'* Journal of Religion in Africa. (1) I 1967 (c).

Turner, Max: *Power fron on High, The Spirit is Israel's Restoration and Witness in Luke-Acts,* Sheffield, SAP 2000.

Others Sources:

AI (Artificial Intellegence, mainly Google)

Okutubo, Femi*: Re Gilbert Deya's 'miracle babies'*
The Trumpet Vol 10 No 5 Sept 1-14, 2004 p2

Vikram, Dodd: *More Children, 'victims of cruel exorcism'*
The Guardian, Saturday, June 4, 2005

About the Author

John Adegoke has been a non-stipendiary Pastor of Cherubim & Seraphim Church in Birmingham, United Kingdom, since 1979. He retired as an Accountant with experience spanning five decades in the UK Civil Service, Food, Education and Engineering Industries.

During his work with the Centre for Black and White Christian Partnership, he acquired immense insight into the theologies of numerous Christian denominations, Black and White, including The Orthodox, Roman Catholic, Protestant, Pentecostal, Charismatic and African Indigenous Churches. He holds a Master Degree in Mission and a Doctorate in Theology.

He has represented the Cherubim & Seraphim Church at various Ecumenical Events, at local, national, and international levels. He is the incumbent Chairman of the Unification of Cherubim & Seraphim Churches, Europe Chapter.